Sex Positions for Couples: 2 Books in 1

Transform Your Sexual Life, Increase Intimacy and

Improve Your Relationship

Marta Zielinska

BOOK 1

Sex Positions

Marta Zielinska

BOOK 1...3

Sex Positions 3

Introduction..8

Erotic Massage 9

Seduction..16

Rules to Observe...24

Foreplay..26

Sexual Positions 32

Sex Positions to Help You Get Over Insecurities 42

Illustrations of Sexual Positions...46

Sex Positions for Advanced 52

Sex Positions for Advanced from Behind....................................59

Various Uses of Sex Toys...68

Oral Sex..72

Anal Sex..73

Common Role Play Scenarios...82

How to Make a Powerful Role Play? 86

Sex Games 90

Advice for Beginners...96

The Challenges of Sexual Education in Society 97

Five Uncommon Facts That Can Improve Your Sex Life 105

Sex Positions for Beginners 109

How to Use Your Hands 118

Have Fun and Play Dirty 125

Spice it up with dirty talks 133

Considerations When Having Sex During Periods 136

Sex in Pregnancy 144

Sex in Overweight 153

Conclusion 162

BOOK 2 164

Sex Guide 164

Make Your Partner Deeply Addicted To You With 164

Secret Tips to Transform Your Sex Life 164

Introduction 167

Orgasm 173

Food for The Soul of Love 183

Romance 185

Foreplay 187

Erotic Games 191

Essential information from the Kamasutra 201

Lubricants, Gels, Toys, and their Role 204

How to Properly Use Lubricants and Gels...211

Sex Toys 213

How To Talk Dirty In An Erotic Way..226

Getting in the Mood...236

Rules of the Game..248

Explore your Sexual Fantasies 264

Fun Masturbation Sessions: Fantasies, Sex Toys, and More 267

What to Stick in Your Ass...275

Fantasies for Couples 279

Ways To Make You Last Longer In Bed 306

Different Sex Positions In A Relationship..315

Conclusion 324

Introduction

The book discusses various ways in which couples could make different positions for ultimate stimulation and intimacy. The first step is also always the easiest; however, which is why the information you find in the following chapters is so essential to take to heart as they are concepts worth learning and practicing.

The initiation of an effective seduction as well as how well to do your foreplay. You will be guided on how to go about the endeavor and make substantial progress, especially if you have difficulties in your sexual life. You will find real-life instances that relate to your situations and experience. You need to acquire this information to enhance your performance in bed while nurturing your relationship. The numerous variants of sex, as well as the positions in which you could enjoy sex, leaves you with a variety of choices that would play a significant role in exploring ways to impress your partner.

Erotic Massage

Our bodies have tremendous capabilities to experience pleasure through the five ordinary senses. Above all, the sense of touch is explored to attain exquisite joy, especially in intimacy. If you are in a loving relationship, erotic massage is a means you could use to stimulate each other. Chiefly, touch and massage is a powerful tool for sexual foreplay. The erotogenic aspect of the human body aids in receiving the tactile massages of desire, love, and tenderness. At the same time, the soul and emotions become nourished.

Benefits of Erotic Massage

Whether you are giving or receiving the massage, you should dissolve into your space and learn to do it without criticism. That way, you rest assured to experience the following benefits from the feeling of touch:

1. ***Facilitates orgasm:*** Erotic massages are mostly meant to cause sexual stimulation. As a result, men experience an erection while women get wet and moody. These are body responses to allow for perfect intercourse.

2. ***Enhances Relationships:*** If you would like to

see your relationship blossom, then you need to incorporate erotic massage in your foreplay. The practice requires you to be emotionally open and conscious. Consequently, you develop a mutual connection that promotes your relationship.

3.   ***Relieves anxiety:*** Your body has endorphin that allows muscle relaxation after the massage. The relaxation helps reduce stress and anxiety, making it a perfect after-work must do.

4.   ***Fights Inflammation:*** Erotic massage is ideal in improving your muscle health and joints. It relaxes and stimulates aching and overworked muscles. Your body becomes flexible and refreshed to proceed with the daily routine.

5.   ***Tone the Skin:*** Erotic massage cleanses your skin by rubbing it gently and unblocking pores. You remain clean as you wipe unwanted layers. Incorporation of massage oil plays a significant role in reviving the natural tone of your skin.

6.   ***Improves Blood Circulation:*** During the massage, the blood flows throughout the body to meet the threshold for sexual stimulation. The heart pumps in moderation as the

relaxation enhances circulation.

7. ***Relaxes Muscles***: As you receive the message, your body experiences gentle and frequent muscle contractions. The process of compressing the muscles is vital in correcting rigid tendons.

8. ***Regulates Hormones***: Massages are known to cause pleasure and stimulation. Specifically, erotic massage helps in boosting your moods and urges. Further, the massage improves your immune system, thus improving the ability to fight infections.

What You Need

Before indulging in the act itself, you should first recall a previous massage session. Create an atmosphere that surpasses what you experienced. In most cases, couples would need to take a warm shower to help relax muscles. The following preparations are crucial in making your room a haven of seduction:

- ***Get Rid of Distractions:*** The most crucial thing about erotic massage is that it works miracles in a quiet and peaceful place. Therefore, you should settle and focused on the activity while avoiding interruptions. Notably, the requirement includes all sorts of distractions, whether physical or psychological.

- *Lighting:* Erotic massage is perfect when done in relatively dim light to create an ethereal atmosphere. For that reason, you should set sources of dim light such as candles to make it warm and cozy. You should apply proper caution as you may be prone to burns.

- *Fragrance:* Scents play a significant role in influencing a person's moods and memories. The application of essential oils and incense sticks provide a therapeutic and pleasant fragrance.

- *Music:* Music is also an important part, especially if it is suitable for erotic massage. It should create a spa atmosphere and should even flow in a sexual and soothing mood.

- *Temperature:* While most couples may prefer a naked erotic massage, the room temperature should be regulated accordingly. You may use a warm sheet to keep your partner comfortable during the massage. Room temperature would be preferable but might be subject to change depending on your adaptation.

How Is It Done?

You should start with gentle touches as you build comfort and confidence with the process. Your partner should help you in deciding whether to start with the hands or feet. The fact that sensual massage acts as foreplay means that you should feel free to seduce your partner. Therefore, you are required to increase physical contact for great feelings of intimacy. Feel free to massage the whole body and pay close attention to nerve endings. The application of techniques serves as a powerful gift that is pleasurable, intimate and demonstrates selflessness.

Types of Erotic Massage

In addition to releasing stress and tension, erotic massage can also help you focus on the pleasurable sensation. In most cases, these forms of massage end up in ejaculation or orgasms.

1. ***Soapy Massage:*** It starts in the shower when naked couples rub soap onto one another. The soap aids in giving a smooth massage as well as cleaning them for further massage or sex.

2. ***Duo Massage:*** It mostly involves two people giving and receiving a luxurious massage. Both the giver and the receiver apply oil on their bodies for a perfect body to body massage.

3. ***Prostate Massage:*** This form of massage aims at stimulating the prostate glands mostly believed to be a man's emotional, sacred, and sexual spot. Stimulated prostate releases psychological and physical pressure that creates an intense experience.

4. ***Lingam Massage:*** It involves honoring the stimulation and sensations

of the penis through massage. It includes gentle touches on the testicles, shaft, and the perineum. It is meant to create sensual stimulation from a thorough genital massage.

5.   ***Yoni Massage:*** Such as the lingam, Yoni involves loving, respecting, and honoring vaginal stimulation through massage. A relaxed yoni massage helps create acceptance of the sexual feelings experienced. This type of erotic massage is beneficial, especially if you want to release sexual issues such as sexual pain and anorgasmia. It is known to build trust and respect in relationships.

Erotic massage is vital in your foreplay, for it allows you to influence your partner's sexual desires. You develop a mutual concept when you exercise different forms of erotic massage. However, you should be careful and deliberate not to mistake a tickle for a massage.

Seduction

Seduction is the act of persuading someone for sexual arousal and intercourse. It mostly happens through actions and words that tend to attract the attention of the victim. If you wish to become a great seducer, you must orchestrate surprise and avoid familiarity and boredom in your relationship. Notably, surprises influence seduction, and it decreases depending on the surprises you make to your partner. For that reason, you will find relationships fading as a result of the lack of surprises among couples. As too many of surprises could be counterproductive, you should create the best moments to make unexpected moves that please your partner. These surprises have power and take much of the victim's afterthought, where they remain glued into it. They build up forms of crystalizing you as a better person.

Unfortunately, seduction is gradually becoming a lost art for people who have become so self-centered that we are unable to analyze the outside perspective. The fact that seduction is a social activity it encourages you to pay attention to feedback and put yourself in other people's shoes. This way, you will learn more about your seductive energy and how to express it adequately.

As a result, you will refine your seduction based on the character that best fits you.

Identify your seduction character: Successful seduction depends on how well you understand yourself and the energy you exert toward the victim. The following categories should guide you and create the best seducer out of you.

- ***Sirens:*** They are physically undeniable, highly sexual, and confident. They are perfect in creating sexual awareness which aids in luring their targets.

- ***Rakes:*** They are highly unrestrained and are ready to let go and become enslaved by the love of women.

- ***Ideal Lover:*** They make their targets feel elevated and deserving success. The character makes the target fall in love by bringing the perfect quality out in them.

- ***Dandies:*** They demonstrate the freedom and limited roles in life. Their confident expression of their lifestyle makes their targets imitate and admire them.

- ***The Natural:*** They practice openness and innocence. The value of retaining the impeccable quality makes them admirable and worthy life partners who would be a relief from the world's guilt.

- ***Coquettes:*** They exercise the power of love and desire, where they portray themselves as self-sufficient. By denying full access, they increase excitement and value, thus more seduction power.

- ***Charmers:*** They are socially friendly and are best in pleasing. The fact that they do not complain or fight influences their seduction.

- ***Charismatic:*** Through their confidence, they create illusions and intense plans that portray them as organized and goal-oriented.

- ***The Star:*** They are ethereal and aim to become an ideal reference when seducing those who are interested in fantasies and dreams. Their appearance makes them identifiable through imaginations.

After analyzing yourself and identifying your category, you will also need to understand your target and maneuvers that will make them surrender. It would be advisable to target those who show a deficiency of your abundance and not try to seduce your type. You should look out for signals of what your target lacks and form the basis of your seduction.

The following are types of seduction targets:

- ***Patient Dreamers:*** They long for exploration and adventure but remain in their boring life.

- ***Reformists:*** They seek to escape custodian sexual life.

- ***Virtual Royals:*** They wish to be treated as special people and live a royal life.

- ***Prudes:*** They like to keep things undercover and would not want you to judge them for their actions.

- ***Dark Stars:*** They once attracted much attention and would like to regain popularity and adoration.

- ***Fresher:*** They consider themselves new to sex life but are ready to explore.

- ***Conquerors:*** They need to be met with plans and missions to overcome.

- ***Exotic Fetishist:*** They are obsessed with exotics and new experiences.

- ***Drama lovers:*** They like to remain fascinated by the happenings and wish to be involved in drama throughout their life.

- ***The intelligent:*** They think and analyze everything profoundly and wish to find help in relieving mental barriers.

- ***The appreciated:*** Used to be praised and needs someone to focus on other aspects that they can enjoy.

- ***Aging Toddlers:*** Portrays immature behavior and needs enabling of the desires and gradually reeling them in.

- ***Life Savers:*** They like to act as your savior by making them believe that you need them as a protector; you make them develop an obsession.

- ***Veterans:*** Their experience in love and sex life makes them desire to educate others.

- ***Idol seekers:*** You must act as an object to provide meaning in life and prompt them to worship you.

- ***Sensualists:*** They rely on what their senses command them. You must master and influence their smell, touch, taste, and sight to win them.

Phases of Seduction

Initially, understand and master your charming character and the perfect target. This way, you will be able to make the moves that will win you a sex partner and companion. Your active seduction should be phased to ensure that you make gradual progress and to allow time for synthesis. By following these phases, you should make an effective seduction that will not only win you the most preferred target but also test your charming character.

Phase 1: Making a Choice: You should choose a victim with voids that you can fill and one who shows notable signs of desperation. Making the right choice includes leaving those who seem inaccessible and hostile as you cannot seduce everyone. Besides, beware of falling prey to those who quickly like you as you may be mistaking insecurity for seduction. Introverts and shy people usually have still waters running deep and are better targeted as compared to extroverts. Your first move should be seeking attention and stirring desire. The step is easy if the target is your friend. In this case, care is not necessary. Develop a friendly conversation on what they like and dislike as a way of knowing them better. Moreover, finding quality time to spend with them is vital as it helps in understanding them and becoming part of their routine. Remember always to remain ambiguous to facilitate the urge of learning your ways and increased interest in you. Ensure that you understand every circumstance that makes your target that they are. Most importantly, understand their reasons for specific courses in life to avoid baseless judgment. In this phase, you must play by your target's rules and adapt to their attitude and moods to avoid strong defense.

Phase 2: Stir it up: This phase mostly involves your actions towards the victim. Ensure that your victim remains in suspense from your activities. Let them wonder what to get next due to your routine innovations and surprises. The feeling gives them the urge to know you better. Surprises make your victim view life as full of new things and places. Therefore, you become the connection between them and the wonderful world and people. Be sure to have the victim engrossed in you, especially if sweet words and promises accompany the surprises. The victim's emotions become inflamed by your fantasies and would find it hard to resist you. Be yourself and restrict your actions based on the tastes of the victim. However, the flavors should not make you hold back your natural traits. Notably, inherent characteristics are the most seductive and could play a significant role in expressing who you are. You only need to create fantasies for your victim and appear to turn her dreams into reality. Most importantly, you will have to emotionally, mentally, and physically move the victim out of their natural environment. It will help break previous connections and establish your relationship through refreshment and adventure.

Phase 3: The Precipice: At this stage, you are in full gear, taking extreme measures, and deepening the effect. Therefore, you should be yourself and should be less worried about making mistakes. You should be ready to act as a rescuer for your victim, even if it means leading them into a crisis. They must believe that you are there for them, and you mean it. You need more in- depth exploration and going beyond the victim's limits to test their submission and also influence their interest. In case your victim has insecurity and doubts about their conscience and sexuality, you could use spiritual lures. It would involve making them focus on the religious experience or other artistic expressions. Chiefly, when you mix pleasure with pain, it positively influences seduction, which should not be unaffected anyway. Simple seduction leads to the fast climax and weak satisfaction, which is contrary to what you need to achieve.

Phase 4: Capture: It is the perfect time where your victim falls on your hand. It happens through acting in a suggestive manner that makes the victim take actions to move closer to you. For instance, you could act interested in someone else and see the victim sense it and react. It is about making the pursued become the pursuer. You should also observe sexual desires that you induce through your glances, voice, and gestures. Trembling of the sound, blushing, and a revealing slip of the tongue are indications that the victim is giving in. Note that you are solely responsible for going on the offensive, ensuring that you maintain your lightness and mystery.

Rules to Observe

Although all couples are different, and each partnership is unique, the following provisions of seduction are applicable in most cases.

- ***Avoid Manipulation:*** Men and women often feel that their partner is fooling them and brings a charged feeling against them. Learn to work with what your partner brings on the table.

- ***Demonstrate independence:*** Develop a dictated passive aggression that requires you to remain in your center, especially when on a first date. Sharing about your world and life makes you more exciting and exciting.

- ***Be natural:*** If you are the target of seduction, you will never know if he/she cares for the real you. Therefore, you need to deal with open people.

- ***Have Fun:*** The natural you should give out the playful part of you to remain attractive and adored.

- ***Be Humorous:*** It makes you sexy if you are able to take both teasers and critics. Also, finding humor indicates that you have a good and sober personality.

- ***Observe Good Hygiene:*** Your breath, appearance, and hygiene may cost you a date no matter how cute you might be. Similarly, you should develop self-esteem to remain proud and secure.

- ***Body Language:*** Your confidence and attitude are visible through your body language. Smile always and avoid flirting with everyone as they may never take you seriously.

You are required to observe patience and perseverance by giving your date a chance to respond. Note that seduction is only in your head and what matters is how others perceive you through your presentation.

Foreplay

Foreplay is an activity at the beginning of a sexual encounter that aims at building sexual arousal and brings orgasm in preparation for sexual intercourse. It is a crucial part of sexual experience and acts as a determinant of satisfaction.

Importance of Foreplay

- ***Biological:*** Couples need to indulge in foreplay, for it causes erection of both; the penis and the clitoris. An erection is crucial for it enhances penetration and orgasm among women. Therefore, it creates the best conditions for biological activity. Besides, foreplay elicits wetness making penetration easier for the couples. Lack of vaginal wetness is associated with painful intercourse and bleeding.

- ***Psychological:*** Foreplay is known to instill a feeling of care and security among couples. Failure to make foreplay makes your partner feel neglected and denied emotional assurance. The concern of your partner's feelings before sex serves as an indicator that you are not in for selfish gains but mutual pleasure.

Types of Foreplay

Foreplay is the ultimate time to build tension and sexual chemistry between partners. If you lack mind-blowing sex, you should focus on foreplay.

Notably, sex is more realistic and complex than what television and movies show. For that reason, when you intimately touch, smell, hear, and taste your partner, they would argue it as better than penetration.

The following are types of foreplay that you should work before sex:

1. ***Sexy Materials:*** You could practice foreplay at any time and manner.

You do not have to be naked to engage in foreplay.
When at home or work, you may watch a sexy movie or
read sexy materials. These materials could help you maintain
orgasm for hours.

2.   *Undressing:* If you usually take off your clothes
before sex, then you might be missing a lot of
foreplay. Having your fingers hold your partner's
outfits and graze on their body as you undress them
is highly stimulating and arousing. Depending on
how sensitive they are, you might witness them
getting goosebumps.

3.   *Vagina stroking:* It involves how you put your
hands down there and caressing on her pants and
panties. Light strokes on the region make her wet
and stimulated for sex.

4.   *Kisses and caressing:* Though kisses do not lead
to sex, most sexual activities involve kisses and
touching. As part of foreplay, kisses should start
slow and intensify gradually. Kisses on the neck
and boobs are most arousing for women.

5.   *Boob Action:* Teases made on their breasts arouse
women. Therefore, you should suck, kiss and rub

them, taking advantage of the sensitive nerve ending in the nipples. The foreplay should be done with moderation to avoid hurting your partner.

6. ***Dry Hump:*** It involves gently grinding on your partner. It can happen when naked to show how moody you are. The foreplay plays a significant role in heating the moment for intercourse.

7. ***Breathing:*** Yes, you are right; your breath arouses and stimulates your partner, especially when done on sensitive areas such as genitals and neck. In this case, bad breath would be counterproductive.

8. ***Hands-On:*** Your hands are a piece of efficient equipment when it comes to foreplay. You should use them to grab your partner's breasts, rub their hair, and thighs. In short, use your hands to explore your partner's body unless they say no.

9. ***Oral:*** If you are okay in giving oral, you should incorporate it into your foreplay routine. Be a little bit gentle by teasing, sucking, and licking the clitoris and allowing time.

10. ***Labia love:*** As a highly ignored part, labia have numerous nerve endings that are perfect for arousal

and stimulation. You can massage them slowly or hold them gently between fingers.

11. ***Ass:*** If you and your partner are into stimulation through the anus, then you should try it out effectively. The most ignored nerve endings in the anus cause sexual stimulation, especially if gently licked.

12. ***Multitask:*** You may incorporate all of these techniques and concurrently make different moves. With the perfect combination, you make your partner fantasized with enjoyable sexual stimulation.

How Do I Give Mind-Blowing Foreplay?

The list of foreplay techniques proves that the activity is a real deal when it comes to sexual arousal. Similarly, mastering the best and most applicable to your partner is a significant step towards sexual satisfaction. You may learn the best technique, but the wrong application of foreplay may be counterproductive to both partners. For that reason, it is advisable to understand the following steps when going for foreplay.

·   ***Relax:*** Although partners have different

timeframes to achieve orgasm, it may take about 3
minutes and twenty minutes for men and women
respectively. So you should take your time and
allow time to climax.

- ***Make it gradual:*** You should start the foreplay
with the areas away from the genitals with slow
stimulation. With hot breaths, kisses, stroking, you
are sure to achieve orgasm once you hit the spot.

- ***Caress gently:*** You should make progressive touches
on the less apparent spots of your partner's body, such
as buttocks and inner thighs. You should delight the
nipples with light feathery touches. In the same way,
you should gradually approach the genitals from the
outer layers as you move inner.

- ***Adjust Stimulation:*** An ongoing touch on nerve
endings reduces their sensitivity. Therefore, you
should vary strokes from light to strong and move
from one spot to another.

- ***Seek Feedback:*** Most partners feel shy, asking for
what they want in foreplay. However, they
appreciate it when asked if they enjoy the foreplay.
With questions like "How does it feel?" there is

good communication and willingness to please a partner. The practice promotes intimacy and enjoyable sex.

- ***Practice:*** You should indulge in foreplay without penetration to know your partner and lead them to repeat orgasms. Continued engagement in other forms of sexual interaction acts as an eye-opener in your sexual horizons.

Sex may hurt if your partner is not ready. Foreplay acts as a preparation for enjoyable sexual intercourse. Ensure that you apply the foreplay that best fits you to avoid accidents and incidents.

Sexual Positions

If you are a novice when it comes to sex, the act can seem really intimidating and overwhelming. When you enter into a sexual relationship, it takes time for you to learn what you like, what your partner likes, and what balance strikes the best chord with you both. Getting tense and worrying about the situation only makes it worse, so my first piece of advice is to take a deep breath and allow yourself to relax. Allow things to move at a natural pace and do not try to rush. Start off with simple positions that are not too challenging so that you can focus on the feelings they arouse. This will allow you to feel connected and safe with your partner. Here are a few simple sex positions that every beginner should try.

You may not have tried tantric sex, but perhaps it's time you did. The idea of Tantric sex goes back generations and the Kama Sutra explained all about it. This was a book written by a priest and the intention of the book was to allow couples to find perfect harmony in their marriages, so that the love lasted longer and the couple found close bonding within their relationship. The same applies today and you can experiment with different lovemaking techniques that enhance your love life. She will love you for it because all of these practices are caring and that's the nature of a woman.

When you decide to try Tantric sex, you will need to have warmed coconut oil for massage that leads to lovemaking. You will also need to prepare the bedroom so that it is a temple of pleasure. Make sure that you protect your sheets with large towels and that you have both discoursed tantric sex in advance. Choose an evening when you have lots of time on your hands and you know you won't be interrupted.

Massage plays a large role in the kind of sexual activity you share with your partner. It's all about satisfying your partner, rather than yourself. Massaging her clitoris isn't all there is to it. Massage inside her and find her G spot. Massage the area of the anus as well if you have both consented to it. You will find that this area actually links with her G spot internally and that you are likely to get a very marked response to this massage. Similarly, she can massage you and the most sensitive area she can massage is the area between the testicles and the back passage because it is here that all of your sexual senses are awakened.

Positions suitable to tantric sex

Closeness and intimacy is everything when you are making love in the tantric way. You may decide that you want to pleasure her in a gentle way and letting her sit on your lap and then sitting up to join her is a good way to start making love. Your bodies will slide together and she will be able to hold onto you or lean back so that you can play with her clitoris as well as entering her vagina. Again, slow rocking will help you to excite each other and you need to learn to hold off on climaxing.

When you feel she is near climax, stop. Then start all over again. The idea of tantric sex is to make the climax something explosive and the more you hold off on climaxing the huger the climax will become. Make sure that you are both on the same page. You can read the Kama Sutra together and try many of the intimate positions suggested, making sure that the climax isn't the whole focus of lovemaking. The focus is on improving the pleasure for your partner and extending that pleasure.

The Bow – This position is a very powerful position and allows full penetration. It also allows a man maximum thrust while a woman's hands can be used to massage the testicles. The woman lies on her back and places her feet onto the chest of her man who is kneeling between her legs. Her behind is raised and you may find it more comfortable if you use a cushion so that the level is perfect for entry into her. Before entering her, make sure that she is massaged and that the oils allow easy penetration. Get her to push against your chest with her feet because this gives you more thrust and more control over the lovemaking process. While you are making love in this way, she can massage you and this helps to make your orgasm even stronger.

Crossed leg lovemaking – This may sound like a contradiction in terms, but it is the position that derives this title because of the stance taken. A man lays his woman onto a table edge. Her legs are lifted to his shoulders but before placing them onto his shoulders, he crosses her legs. You may wonder why the crossing of the legs is so essential but this is because of the woman's anatomy. It gives her greater control over the muscles within the vagina and she is able to move her body in rhythm with his so that she gains maximum thrust and he gains maximum friction. It's a wonderful way to make love and something that will make both the man and the woman very happy indeed.

If you introduce tantric sexual practices into your lovemaking, you will find that you will be less shy of each other and will be able to share a lot more of your desires with your partner as well as being open to listen to hers. She may have a wealth of ideas that will spice up your love life, but she needs to have total trust in your reactions. Be open and talk to her. Let her know that the rules of the bedroom are that she can feel free to talk about her own sexual desires as well as fulfilling yours. Many women are a little shy about talking about sex, so will need that level of reassurance that helps them to open up and be honest. It isn't lack of honesty. It's being afraid of your reactions that make a woman hold back from being adventurous. Show her that you want her to be happy in bed and listen to what she says. She may have ideas that will fill your lovemaking with a new sense of happiness and contentment.

If you are a novice when it comes to sex, the act can seem really intimidating and overwhelming. When you enter into a sexual relationship, it takes time for you to learn what you like, what your partner likes, and what balance strikes the best chord with you both. Getting tense and worrying about the situation only makes it worse, so my first piece of advice is to take a deep breath and allow yourself to relax. Allow things to move at a natural pace and do not try to rush. Start off with simple positions that are not too challenging so that you can focus on the feelings they arouse. This will allow you to feel connected and safe with your partner. Here are a few simple sex positions that every beginner should try.

Missionary Position

This position is famous for its simplicity and the great variation that it allows for both partners. By simply changing the angle of your legs, you can change the sensations aroused from this position. It allows for a deep feeling of connection between partners while allowing deep penetration. It is also one of the most common positions that allow women to orgasm from penetrative sex. This is due to the fact that the man's penis is more likely to hit the woman's g-spot with inward strokes of his penis. To get started with the basic missionary position, the woman lies on her back and the man gets into position between her spread thighs so that their pubic regions are aligned and penetration is possible.

Lying Face to Face

This position is great for beginners as it allows you to both be comfortable and be in tune with each other's needs because of the intimacy it creates due to the eye contact and deep penetration. To do this position, all you have to do is lie on your sides facing each other. The woman should lie slightly higher than the man with her hips above his. She should then place her top leg over his hips and allow his penis to slide inside of her.

Spooning

This position is great for G-spot stimulation and allows for lots of skin-to-skin contact. It is like cuddling and sex in one. The man can easily reach around and stimulate the woman's clit in this position. This is a simple position for couples to achieve. Lay in a spooning position with the woman's hips slightly above the man's. Her top leg should be slightly lifted so that he can penetrate her.

Woman on Top

In this position, the woman straddles the man while he sits so that their faces are close together. This position allows the woman more control but still allows the couple to be connected emotionally. To get in this position, the man must be seated and reclined against something like a couch or a wall. The woman straddles him until their genitals are aligned and penetration is possible.

Doggy Style

This position is great for deeper penetration and leaves both the man's and woman's hands-free for clitoral play and stimulation. To get into this position, the woman rests on her hands and knees with her legs spread so that her partner can get behind her. She can adjust the width of her legs closer or wider to accommodate height differences and to allow for the variations in penetration.

Experimental Sexual Positions for Beginners

Variety is the spice of life, and this is also true for sex. Doing the same positions over and over again can quickly become boring and make a couple's sex life become stagnant. This does not have to happen to you and your partner. Even if you are both beginners to sex, you can switch things up and keep things spicy with the position outlined below.

Missionary Position Variations

Remember that I said that the missionary position allows for great versatility. By lifting the woman's feet off the bed and pushing her knees closer to her chest, this variation in the missionary position allows for deeper penetration and greater access to the G-spot. If the woman is particularly limber, she can place her ankles on the man's shoulders for an even greater lift of her buttocks off the surface that they are lying on.

You can also alter the missionary position by placing a pillow underneath the woman's hips. This missionary variation allows the man's body to rub against the woman's clitoris with every inward stroke of his penis. This makes the woman more likely to orgasm from the position.

In the missionary position, you can also experiment with the woman lifting one leg at a time and having the man lift his chest at different angles away from her body. Small things can make a huge difference, and the variations that you can add to the missionary position are a testament to that fact.

Modified Doggy Style

This position is great for participating in dirty talk as the man's mouth is close to the woman's ear. In this position, the woman lies on her stomach with her hips tilted towards the man who lies behind her. A pillow under the woman's hips can allow the couple to find the right angle for pleasurable penetration. In addition, this is a great position for a woman who would like to show off her derriere to her partner if it is a feature that she is proud of.

Dangling Over the Bed

This position is easy on a man's body as it does not require him to hold his body up with his arms. Since the woman is lying on the edge of a bed with her legs hanging off, he simply has to place himself between her thighs, penetrate her, and thrust them both to a happy finish.

Sex Positions to Help You Get Over Insecurities

Having body issues and feeling insecure about your body is not something that is new, and both men and women suffer from the condition that can sometimes be debilitating. These insecurities can, of course, transfer into your sex life as you need to bare your body to have good sex. The great thing about having a supportive sex partner is that they can help you get over these insecurities and perceived flaws since most of the time we are a lot harder on ourselves and see flaws that other people do not.

Of course, you can help get over these insecurities by addressing them in individual ways such as going to the gym and dieting if you feel that you are overweight. In the bedroom, to help get over your insecurities, a great technique is to find the positions that highlight the features you find most attractive about yourself.

Before we look at some of the sex positions that will allow you to feel less insecure about your body, there are a few other things that you can do to boost your self-confidence in your physical appearance:

- Learn to love yourself and build your self-esteem. No matter the sexual positions that you try, if, at the end of the day, you do not love yourself for who you are and what you look like, your insecurities will always rear their head.

- Spend more time naked. Get familiar with what it feels like to be naked and become intimate with your own body so that when it comes time to be sexually intimate with your partner, you are less likely to be uncomfortable in your own skin.

- Disassociate with people who speak negatively to you about you. Associating with toxic people who not only talk negatively about your body but about their own has a negative impact on you. Therefore, if you have people like this in your life, it is time to have a frank and open discussion about how their words affect you, and if they are not willing to change, then you need to think about cutting them out of your life.

Without further ado, here are a few sexual positions that will encourage you to have a better body image about yourself:

Cowgirl

This position is great for helping you get over insecurities because it brings any issues that may be had to the forefront so that they can be dealt with. For example, if a woman is insecure about her breasts, in this position her partner has a full view of them and can reassure her of her beauty and uniqueness. This is also a great position for a woman who feels that her breasts are one of her best assets and wants to show them off to her partner.

This position is great for beginners because it provides body views and great eye contact. To get into this position, the woman straddles her partner and guides his penis to penetrate her. She should use her hands and knees for balance. She bounces her hips up and down to provide stimulation to both herself and her partner. The man can aid this by lifting his hips up and down as well and supporting her with his arms. In this position, the woman can control the speed and intensity of the strokes. She can also widen her knees or bring them closer to change the depth of penetration.

The Three-Legged Dog Position

This position is great for the promotion of dirty talk and having eye contact in addition to having full upper body contact. It allows both partners to concentrate on their emotional connection rather than physical appearances. Therefore, it is great for people with insecurities since the emphasis is placed on eye contact rather than on each other's bodies. This position involves both parties standing. To aid with equilibrium, one party can lean against a wall. The woman leans into the man with her legs separated and hikes one leg over his hips so that he can penetrate her.

In a Chair

This position is great for reassuring insecurities for the same reasons that the above position is. It allows for lots of upper body contact and lots of eye contact. In this position, the man sits in a chair and the woman straddles him with her thighs on either side of his body. She can bounce up and down or grind against him to stimulate them both.

Lotus

In this position, the man sits crossed-legged on a flat, comfortable surface, and the woman sits on his lap so that they are facing each other. She wraps her legs and arms around him. They can both aid in the penetration and stimulation of each other. This position helps both parties feel secure in the fact that they are emotionally connected with eye contact. Just like the spooning position, this is sex and cuddling in one, and all the associated feel-good hormones are released when couples engage in sex in this position.

Illustrations of Sexual Positions

Missionary 180

Pressed Missionary

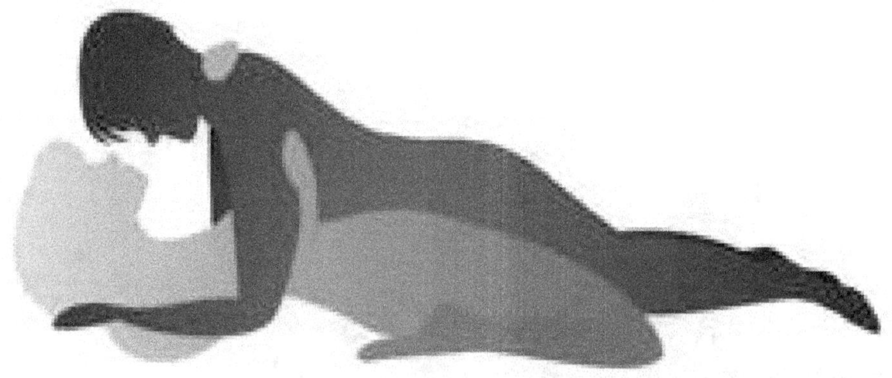

Being an enthusiastic sex position among the family of missionary sex position, it is quite amazing and marvelous. The woman lies straight with her back on the ground and legs bent on the knees, heading back towards her abdomen, providing full exposure of her holes to her partner. On the other hand, the man lies on top of her body, with face right in front of her face, providing enthusiastic kissing and licking experiences for both partners. The man caresses her hair or shoulders with his hands while the woman pushes him towards herself to ensure reddish physical contact. Being exposed in this position, woman allows her partner to go deep inside her vagina or anal hole, providing mild sex experience and unforgettable moments for both. This position allows the man to go harder on his female partner by strongly aiming and pushing to go deep inside the depths of the vagina or anal hole. Anal inclusion could be more interesting for the couple as it offers more pleasures through anal gaping.

Crabby Groundhog

Another enthusiastic sex position from the family of man on top sex positions is crabby groundhog. It entails the woman lying straight on her abdomen and upper body lifted by bending elbows. The man sits on her pelvis, reclining backward into a crab position. This position seems a bit difficult for men who find it to be straining. This straining causes you to pain in the lower back. These drawbacks can be reduced by placing a few pillows under the women's pelvis and making the angle of penetration more horizontal. This horizontal angle might become easier to go for strong stimulation, strong bumping, and a bit shallow penetration. This position allows clitoral stimulation due to the rubbing of the penis with vaginal lips. Thus, makes it an amazing and mild experience for both partners. Going into anus hole of your partner could be difficult because of tilted angle and less availability. If you wanna try some tricky sex with an adventurous ride, you must try this with your partner.

Pressed Wrapped Bull

If you wanna try an adventurous delight applauded with sensational kissing, licking and physical stimulated response, then you must try pressed wrapped bull once. It requires you and your lady to be stretchy enough to perform it in the best way, but it's worth it. It has the power to steer the partners towards their self. The woman lies on the ground with her back and her pelvis is lifted by the man in order to place it in his lap. Her legs are bent on her knees, heading backward. While the man sits on the ground with his legs driven apart to accommodate her body between his legs. He is reclined forward on his woman to suck her boobs, lick her body and kiss her gently to spice up the sexual intercourse. Sex with these prerequisites becomes delightful and habitual. This position allows the man to go inside the vagina and anal hole up to his choice or according to his lady's will. Meanwhile, she can feel every inch of the penis, shattering her holes to go deep inside and make a pleasurable passageway. Squeezing her boobs while penetrating her as fast as you can add enough excitement to transform you both into wild beasts.

Planted Wrapped Bull

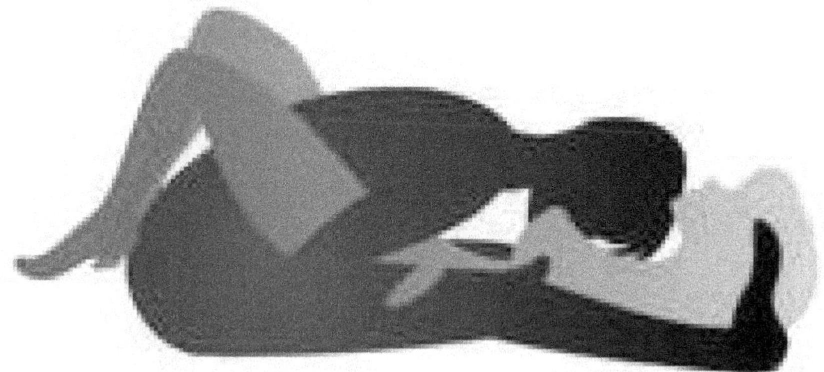

Planted wrapped bull is another enthusiastic sex experience out of the class of man on top and bull variations. This is quite fantastic due to its approach and delightful experience. In this position, the woman lies on the ground with her back and her pelvis aligned with her partner's penis. Her legs are bent and lifted above the ground by her man who uses his hands to push her towards himself to ensure deeper penetration and stronger stimulations. The man sits on the ground with straight legs driven apart to accommodate her body and leaned forward to kiss her boobs, abdomen, shoulders, and lips. He can thoroughly lick her body to replenish the sexual intercourse and turn sex into a mild experience. With every strong bump, his penis visits the depths of the vagina or anal hole and fills him with filthy affection. The more hard he goes, the more plausible it will be to have sex with full intent.

Sex Positions for Advanced

Woman on Top

Lying Rodeo

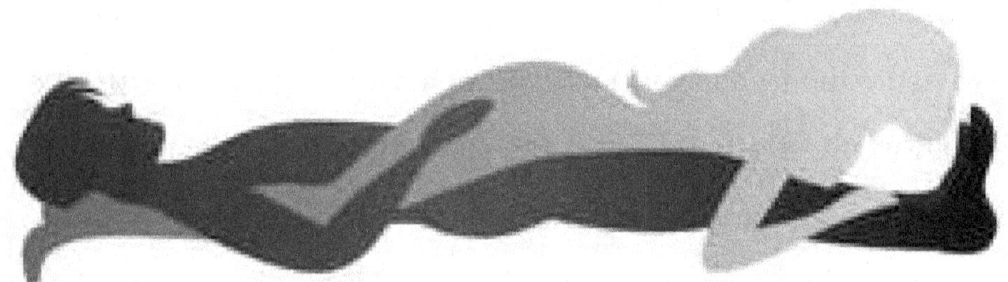

A profound sex position with women on top, giving her the dominance and respect over her male partner is famously known as lying rodeo. This shows extremism to leaning forward, as the woman lies on her abdomen on the legs of her man, with her pelvis right above the penis of the man, who is lying straight on the ground, and allowing easy vaginal intercourse. If you love to give foot job, then this position is made absolutely for you. More attention and consideration should be required for the penile angle as penetration wouldn't be straight forward. For men, this position could be a little difficult as it is slow to the start but offers many enthusiastic dealings and full exposure of her holes. The men can see every inch of his penis going inside her holes. This might be a little tricky for men but amazing for women who can control the penis inclusion as well as the bumping speed.

Arched Cowgirl

This is quite an amazing yet classical position as it belongs to the most favorite cowgirl sex positions family. In this position, the man lies on his back with straight legs. While the women, being on top, kneels over him, arched backward and sustains herself with hands on the floor. This position allows the women to move and haul according to her choice and will. Therefore, the majority of the movement in this position comes from the women lifting, rocking, bumping hardly and rotating her hips. The man puts his hands on her thighs and caresses her legs to stimulate her joys and plausible pleasures. The second variation is playing with her breasts, which will not only stimulate her sex experience to mildness but also indulge both thoroughly in sex. This position also offers a treat of sight-seeing of penis inclusion to her holes. Frictionless inclusions with both vaginal and anal intercourse are guaranteed to delight both partners. The more intense you are to try this position, the more joyous it will be for you and your partner. Being an advanced yet easy sex position, this can be easily performed every time you like.

Planted Arched Cowgirl

Anastasiia Frizen - © 123RF.com

Yet another enthusiastic treat from the family of cowgirl and woman on top is planted arched cowgirl. This position is an extension of the arched cowgirl. It involves the man, lying on the ground with the upper body lifted, that sustains himself with fists on the floor. While the woman, being on top, sits on his abdomen, arched backward just like in the arched cowgirl position. This position allows the man to not only explore the sight-seeing of penis inclusion but also delights him with clitoral playing and stimulate her nerves to go wild towards the sexual approach. On the other hand, the woman opens her legs wide apart to give him full access, together with deeper penetration and frictionless inclusion. Woman, being on top, is captivated with controls over penetration and movements according to her choice. The movements mostly come from her side when she lifts, rocks and rotates her hips. Both partners, in this position, can catch each other's emotions and move in a rhythm that will bring more satisfaction for both of them.

Bridged Cowgirl

Anastasiia Frizen - © 123RF.com

One of the adventurous and enthusiastic positions from the cowgirl family is bridged cowgirl. This is unique according to its approach and sex experience. It involves the man settling down with bouncy abdomen, lifting while touching the ground with hands. On the other hand, the woman, being on top, sits on his abdomen, facing towards his head and praising him with her weight. This position allows deeper penetration and strong stimulation together with frictionless inclusion. It goes really hard for the male partner as he is not able to see going through and feel much difficulty in maintaining this position while lifting the weight of his women too. On the other hand, women can also not freely bounce on the penis because of her feet not touching the ground and letting her balance her body by herself. This position offers less intensity with less movement and hence, lesser satisfaction and joys.

Facedown Cowgirl

Anastasiia Frizen - © 123RF.com

Yet another furious and adventurous sex position from the family of cowgirl and woman on top sex positions is facedown cowgirl. This position entails the man lying straight, with straight legs on the bed and upper body inclined downward with shoulders touching the ground and supporting his body. On the other hand, the woman sits on his penis at the cutting edge of the bed and balances her body being arched backward and hands-on bed to support her body leaning backward. This position offers complete control and movements assigned to the woman. She can control the penetration angle as well as the penetration length. The more she settles her down, the more penis length will be included in both of the holes. The man can caress her legs and play with her clit to spice up the sex experience, even if can't play with her boobs. Playing with her clit could bring more joys for both of them that will indulge them deeply and forever.

Sex Positions for Advanced from Behind

Planted Sinner

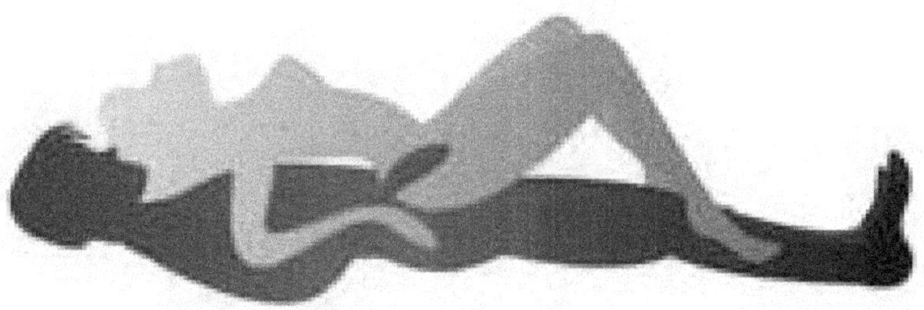

An amazing position belonging to the family of sex from behind is planted sinner. In this variation of sex, the man lies straight on the floor with legs fully straighten; whereas, the woman is lying on his body facing away from his face to give behind ways sex, while her legs are planted closer to the action. Man sustains the woman by her hips and provides her finer control over her pelvis that lies above the penis. He can go through the anal hole with heavy frictions and therefore guarantee anal gaping. While for vaginal intercourse, this seems a bit difficult as vagina lies a bit above and therefore it guarantees strong stimulation and rubbing with the inner lips of the vagina. This position allows less deep penetration with strong rubbing and enthusiastic sexual intensity. Both partners can indulge in sex too hard by going wild in kissing and licking her lips, face and neck. A gentle approach could drive both partners towards the crazy world of extreme sexual intercourse.

Planted Amazon 180

This is another amazing sex position belonging to the family of sex from behind and quite similar to amazon 180 variation. Is also known as the backpack sex position. It involves the

woman on her feet, facing away from the man, giving him full

penile exposure to her holes and allowing him to go in the hole

of his choice. She opens her legs to give room to her partner

and, on the other hand, the man places his feet on her back to

sustain her at the right spot. The best thing about this position

is that she sits on his penis allowing him to go deep and feel

every inch of vaginal depth and anal gaping together with full

back exposure and pleasurable sight-seeing of the penis going

deep inside the holes. While for woman, as she is sitting on the

penis, she can decide how much length of the penis to digest

and in which hole, making this position perfect for women that

like to have control. Sensible and enthusiastic sex with mildness and furiousness is guaranteed in this sex position to delight both partners with satisfaction.

Folded Amazon 180

Anastasiia Frizen - © 123RF.com

This is another variation from the family of amazon sex positions and sex from behind family and is commonly known as folded amazon 180. This involves the woman sitting on his lap to allow thorough access of the penis for both the vagina and anal hole. She sits with kneeling legs while the man lies straight on the ground with kneeling legs and hands on her ass to sustain her body. On the other hand, the woman places her hands on his knees to support her body. As the woman sits on his penis, this position guarantees strong stimulation with extravagant penile attributions and deeper penetrations. However, the woman can control the length of the penis going inside by lifting her ass up. She can spice up her feelings and sensuality by going hard with rocking, lifting and tilting her ass sideways to allow fractioned stimulation and extreme sex experience together with mildness and extreme sexual intent.

Fire Hydrant

Anastasiia Frizen - © 123RF.com

Plausible and amazing sex experience is guaranteed in fire hydrant sex position. A marvelous experience is guaranteed with the woman lifting her one leg straight up and out sideways. While the other leg is used to sustain herself on the elbow. The man stands on his knees right behind her pelvis to aim straight at the vagina and supports her straighten leg by his hand while the other hand is placed on her ass to caress her body. This position allows strong bumping and stimulation together with harsh going and deeper penetrations as no friction and hurdles come in the way to the vagina. The harsher you aim at the vagina, the deeper it will be included inside and up to every inch of the penis. The woman feels the intent and loves to enjoy the fuller length of the penis shattering her hole and deeply delighting her sex experience. This is quite a marvelous sex position if tried with a pillow right beneath her folded knee. It requires a little bit of stamina by the woman side to be performed, but it offers enormous rewards.

Supported Aerial Doggy

Anastasiia Frizen - © 123RF.com

A pretty amazing and marvelous sex position, belonging to the group of sex from behind, is supported aerial doggy sex. This position seems a bit difficult for men having a thin body figure and leaned muscles. This is a versatile sex position and favored by many. The man's body is lifted and sustains himself by his hands placed on the bed, with legs straight backward lying in the air. Advanced level sex freaks more often to visit this enthusiastic sexual intercourse as it involves mildness and craziness. The woman would feel a lot more comfortable in this sex position when thrusting harder and with stronger intent to go deep inside the vaginal hole. Going with anal gaping could be a feast for joy and enjoyment as the anal hole is nearer and could be shattered with less power. The harsher you go on with bumping to your lady, the more sensible it will be.

Standing Squatting Rodeo

Anastasiia Frizen - © 123RF.com

Another amazing position from the family of sex from behind is standing squatting rodeo. This involves the woman sitting on the man's penis with legs folded and leaned on the bench or bed where they are experiencing sexual intercourse. Moreover, the woman sustains herself on feet, that are placed near the body on the bench or bed. On the other hand, the man lies straight on the bench with legs folded on the knees and rested feet on the ground. The more intense you aim at the vagina, the deeper it will be, but it requires the placement of the vaginal hole right above the penis to guarantee frictionless and deeper penetration. If you go soft with tilted angles or different angles expect right above the penis, the inclusion will not be great, as it will bend the penis and due to the resting of woman's ass on the penis of the man. This position is quite amazing, sensible, enthusiastic and fantastic for every frequent sex freak to indulge deep and turn your partner towards yourself with a little effort to reward you more.

Various Uses of Sex Toys

Normalize Sensitivity: Partner may have difficulties having intercourse due to their bodies being hypersensitive. It is a common scenario among new couples. Their genitals may not be exposed to sex before and require preparations for the real act. Sex toys could be used slightly to stimulate the genitals, and they will be ready to have sex with time.

Foreplay: Sex toys are best in causing stimulations, especially for couples, for they are multipurpose and continuous. Partners could use the different types of toys to stimulate each other before they engage in actual sex. It would work miracles for less physically fit couples. It also saves time that partners could take to achieve stimulation.

Maintain Stimulation: Sex toys do not disappoint when incorporated in sex. They may be used to cause stimulation to both partners making sex more pleasurable. When using sex positions that have limited caressing and kissing, sex toys could be the ultimate solution.

Prolong Stimulation: In this case, the partners wish to prolong the stimulation even after orgasm and sex. As they relax after sex, couples could continue using the toys to make the stimulation last longer. It could work for men with erectile dysfunction, for it aids in a prolonged erection.

Third Partner: Sex toys could be used in case one of the partners has passed out or cannot reach certain sensitive areas. For instance, a partner would prefer concurrent stimulation on both the anus and the vagina. The sex toys would take one responsibility as the partner handles the other.

With all these uses, you are sure to find the best sex toy that will work for you and your partner. There are few evitable cons of sex toys while the pros make them a must use.

Pros of Sext Toys

1. ***Enhances Body Knowledge:*** The use of sex toys during sex helps partners explore each other bodies and understand the part with more sensory stimulation.

2. ***Enhances Sexual Pleasure:*** The combination of these toys with sex provides additional pleasure.

3. ***Self Confidence:*** While using sex toys, you are sure that sexual stimulation is guaranteed, making you aim at attaining satisfaction.

4. ***Quick Orgasm:*** The hyper intensive stimulation caused by sex toys reduces the time a partner would require to attain an orgasm. For that reason, sex starts at the right time with little effort applied.

5. ***Control Sexual Needs:*** Sex toys could be used by either partner for sexual stimulation.

6. ***Fosters Love:*** The exploration of your partner's

genitals as well as communication as you try out sex toys removes barriers and enhances mutual connections.

7. **Prevents STIs:** The use of sex toys means that genitals may not need to make contact, thus preventing the spread of sexually transmitted Infections.

8. **Improves Performance:** The sensitivity associated with sex toys boosts the partner's morale, making them perform above par.

9. **Prevents Unwanted Pregnancy:** The fact that sex toys do not ejaculate makes it safe for the woman from impregnation.

1. **Toxicity:** Materials used to make sex toys may be toxic to your body, although few severe cases have come up.

2. **Infections:** Untidy and contaminated devices may

carry bacteria that may end up infecting your body.
For that reason, you should ensure that your sex
toys are kept safely in a clean environment.

Oral Sex

This form of sex involves the use of the mouth to stimulate
the external reproductive organs of your partner. It goes well
when combined with sucking, nibbling, blowing, and licking.
Fellatio is when a man is receiving oral sex, and *cunnilingus* is
oral sex on a woman. In fellatio, the giver of oral sex uses the
mouth to stimulate the penis and the scrotum of the man.

On the other hand, cunnilingus involves using the mouth to
stimulate the clitoris, vulva, and the openings of the vagina.
Besides, oral sex done on the anus is called *analingus*. It is worth
noting that using the mouth to stimulate other body parts such
as the lips and breasts is not oral sex. Nevertheless, oral sex is
an enjoyable and intimate practice for sexy couples. There has
been so much misinformation and mystery surrounding this
form of sex that it is amazingly punishable in some
jurisdictions. For that reason, you should understand oral sex
and decide on whether to make it part of a romantic

relationship.

Anal Sex

It is a form of sex where the penetration occurs at the anus. The practice happens intending to cause sexual stimulation and play. Therefore, it does not have to end in penetration necessarily. The play may involve stimulating the rectum, bum, or the anus. Note that this form of sex should not be a goal for you to achieve but a pleasure that you choose. Tickling or massaging the outer part of the butt hole is also considered as anal sex, for it offers stimulation and delight just as other forms of sex. There are various ways you could stimulate your partner through the anus, and it can be concurrent for both of you. By mastering the following common anal sex positions, you gain additional knowledge on how to get down on your partner.

Anal Sex Positions

Missionary: This position mostly involves deep penetration as the man is on top of the woman. The position offers double stimulation if the woman is another male. There are numerous variations of this technique, and the man remains in control of pace, rhythm, and depth of penetration. The woman could raise the hip to enhance position the partners face the same direction while lying on a flat platform. The man enters from behind, forming a spoon shape. In this case, the woman remains in full control of the intercourse. This position offers added stimulation as hands are free to caress and maintained a complete body contact.

Doggy: It can be performed with both partners kneeling or standing. The woman may bend to expose the anus for the man who stands erect behind. It offers a clear view of the penetration and reduces obstruction from the rest of the body. The partners may support each other to avoid falling off. The man may hold the woman's waist as the holds ion a chair.

Receiver on Top: *as* the name states, this position has the woman on top of the man. It leaves more control to the woman who decides what pace, speed, and depth to achieve. The man lies on a flat platform, and the only effort he could apply is raising the hips to penetrate deeper or make thrusts. They may decide to take different variations which may diversify the level of stimulation.

Posture seven: It is a position you are likely to find in manuals depicting the posture made in sex from behind. The woman lies on a flat platform allowing the man to straddle the lower leg and lift it to his elbow or shoulders. This position makes the partners make a posture similar to number seven. Although most couples find this position as acrobatic, others perceive it as comfortable, especially if they have health problems or concerns.

Best Practices for Safe Anal Sex

There are various ways in which you could explore anal sex. The variance makes couples curious about positions and penetration. If you are ready to find out ways to explore anal play safely and pleasurably, you should exercise these steps:

Research: If you are reading this point, you are on the right track of perfecting in anal sex. It is advisable to understand the organs involved to make the right decisions and moves. Specifically, you should understand the pressure — the reaction of your anus as well as that of your partner. You should also understand the occurrence of stimulation occurs after the application of pressure on the ventral walls of the anus

Take Easy: If you are new to anal play and sex, you should take it slow and avoid rushing for orgasm. Time is of the essence as you explore the prostate gland, anal canal, and the sphincter muscles. You should help each other understand what works and what fails. If you feel overwhelmed by negative and stressful emotions, you should relax and breathe out. Notably, the pain might be a sign that something is wrong.

Communicate: Your partner should be ready to try out the new technique before you bump on them for a quickie. It includes opening your mind and communicating your feelings and suggestions, trying the unique experience. If they are in for it, ensure you combine it with caressing and other fantasy, for it does not only involve penetration.

Be Safe: Anal sex is not a rush thing and requires proper preparations before penetration. The anus requires caution as you insert relatively larger objects. It is advisable to start with your finger as you gradually adjust sizes and observing the reaction. Ensure that the objects you put in the anus have a flared base to prevent them from being sucked into the rectum. Chiefly, most beginners incorporate effective lube to make it safe and comfortable.

Cleanliness: The taboo aspect of anal sex makes it more arousing for couples. For that reason, they believe that sex must be dirty to be considered effective. However, if you are engaged in anal sex, some aspects will need extra care. Direct contact of the anal fluids and the vagina may transfer bacteria that inhabit the anus. You could use a latex condom to avoid this direct contact or wash thoroughly before penetration.

Pros of Anal Sex

Immunity: In general, sex offers fantastic health benefits. Specifically, anal sex boosts your immune system, for it aids in blood circulation as you are involved in sexual exercises. The physical fitness makes you remain in good shape and introduce antibodies that fight off other conditions.

Appeal: Anal sex offers a stimulating appeal on men's prostate as well as the vagina. The nerve endings in these areas are more likely to come into contact with the groin of the man. Consequently, the sensitivity makes the partner experience the appeal and enjoy the intercourse.

Nerve Ending: This form of sex seeks to explore the nerve endings found in the anus. The partners can compare the sensitivity as well as the degree of stimulation possible. This way, the partners can decide on making various forms of sex, depending on their preference.

Clearing: The penetration of a penis or any other object in the anus is likely to clear the way out for excretion as a form of sex, anal sex aids in bowel movement keeping the woman healthy. Rubbing of the anus increases the blood flow enhances standard blood pressure and digestion.

Pleasure: The fact that reproduction is rare in anal sex makes it solely for fun. Men enjoy sex for the find the anus as tighter as compared to other openings such as the vaginal or the mouth. It also makes them feel dominant and rebellious, a sense that feeds their instincts. Women enjoy anal sex due to the sensitivity of the nerve endings around the anus. They also experience stimulation in their clitoris if men use the missionary position for anal sex.

Intimacy: Before anal sex happens, the partner must have had mutual trust and transparency. Partners have nerve, insecurity, and privacy issues when it comes to giving in for anal sex. This form of sex requires partners to put aside their reputation and physical requirements. The men treat it as an unusual step by the woman to please him. The women take it as a man's way to show that they are ready to explore them.

Contraceptive: Practicing means that you have no plans to get kids. Similarly, you may use this form of sex when your partner senses that she may get pregnant. It is meant to put out the tension among women reliving them for a great and pleasurable session ahead.

Beneficial Semen: exposure to semen reduces the chances of contracting breast cancer and nausea, and the same case applies in anal sex. When the fluid comes into contact with the woman's body, they are likely to cause increased energy, reduces stress, increased libido, and mental alertness.

Diversity: Anal sex has incorporated different aspects that are interesting to people who felt bored with sex. Partners find this form of sex as a way to introduce something new in their relationship and sex life. It is the best solution for long term relationships partners who would like to make things fun.

HPV: You might be infected with HPV as you engage in anal sex. The virus may lead to cancer of the anus.

HIV: Although anal sex prevents pregnancy, it does not on the side of STIs. If you fail to use protection, you may pass or contract HIV from your partner.

Prolapsed Anus: Although it is a rare occurrence, practicing hardcore sex may be hazardous for you or your partner.

Poop: Anal sex is associated with coming into contact with fecal matter. However, this should not come as a surprise, and you should learn how to deal with the issue sexually.

Role Play

Role play involves sexual advancements and moves. It also includes two or more people who act different characters with sexual enticement. The play targets a specific audience and is best for people struggling in sexual life. Nonetheless, it is more pleasurable when made ordinary and sexy. The variant has fantasies that take the targets to their dreams of joy and pleasure. Notably, the effects created in role-play start from the imagination of the real you and desires. The nature of the role play solely depends on the partners involved and what they deem sexy. They may wear different costumes to play about scenarios that their partners find sexy and seductive. The following are common scenarios performed in role play.

Common Role Play Scenarios

Slave: This form of play has one partner comply with all the orders of the "master" who now is the dominant partner. It makes the masters feel dominant, arousing their nerve and the sexual hormones.

Teacher: The scenario applies s logic similar logic as that of the slave, but in this case, the woman acts as a student. The dominant partner works teacher and is flee to 'punish' the student.

Doctor-Patient: It has the dominant partner acting to 'treat' the submissive partner who works as a patient. The submissive partner may work as either nurse or patient provided they apply medical fetishism.

Boss: It is also known as the executive for its workplace setting. It involves the submissive partner acting as the secretary of the boss, who, in this case, is the dominant partner.

Escort: One partner acts as the superiors of the other who works as a security escort. It also follows the ideology of superiority and submission.

Handy Man: The role play is acted out by a technician who came to do some repairs. After accessing the housewife's home, they develop sexual interests, and he submits to her.

Photographer. It involves partners taking photos of each other and making sexual gestures. The act is mostly laid out to serve as a precursor to romantic sex after that.

Stripper. The role play is self-explanatory as the name states. It is merely a partner stripping to seduce the other for sexual arousal and eventually sex.

Gender play: in this role play, partners take roles of a different gender. They act out as the opposite gender and entice their partners and instill an imagination in them.

Animal: Most partners who submit to this role play receive less humane treatment and compared with pony, cat, or a dog. They submit to any position or advancement.

Owner: Dominant partners act as a homeowner, and the submissive partner acts as an object such as a table or cupboard.

Age Play: Partners pretend to be of different ages, and one appears to submit due to age difference. Most pretend to be young and enhance regression.

Supernatural: In this role play, one partner takes the roles of succubus, or vampires to dominate their partners. It is a compelling presentation where the victim appears feeble and helpless.

Uniform: The partners in this role play wear uniforms to match specific characters such as students and French maid. One of the partners may choose to act dominant by acting teacher or boss or put on a uniform to be a companion.

Incest: The name comes from the notion that partner in this role play makes. They take roles to appear related and making sexual moves.

Police: In this case, one partner acts as a law enforcement officer while the submissive one acts as a lawbreaker. The dominant partner humiliates and blackmails the partner to sexual activity.

You could also try bout these role-play as you seek to add color and pomp to your love life. Besides, you should take measures for a well-done role play.

How to Make a Powerful Role Play?

1. ***Identify your fantasies***: Think about what drives you crazy in your life. Is it the hot DJ in the club? Is it your dentist? You may be wishing for a full naked massage. If you have read erotic fiction or watched sexy materials, you may have had a hint of what these fantasies are. These imaginations are crucial in role-playing, for it is limited to that.

2. ***Discuss:*** You could explain your fantasy depending on the character you choose. Gauge the interest by emphasizing the illusion that you see.

3. ***Kinky***: Notably, most of the role plays involve superiority. For that reason, it would be advisable to make it kinky. You do not have to be necessarily aggressive but safe.

4. ***Take Slow***: People who rush their role play make their partners find it silly. Therefore, you should take your time if you are turned on by playing pretend.

5. ***Costumes:*** Make the best selection of the role you choose by making the best of the character. On the contrary, you could decide to undress if that is the sexier character.

Pros of Role Play

Enhances Communication: Role-playing involves making a body language to pass a message to your partner. This aspect makes it a powerful tool of communication.

Enhances Trust: The acting out of fantasies in role-play can only happen if partners feel secure and safe. Therefore, it shows that couples are free and confident of each other.

Foreplay: Normally, most role-plays end up in sex. Therefore, it would be advisable to try out the play if you want to have intimate sex.

Healing: One of the hidden treasures of role-playing is the healing effect it has on partners. A relieving role play switches partner who is down.

Educative: Taking the character of someone else and acting like them requires a certain level of intellectual capacity. It helps you learn different gestures and understandings.

Enticing: The sexy gestures associated with role-playing are inevitable. They take away the conscious of the target and take them to the illusion world.

Safety: Roleplaying is one of the safest variants of sex fort involves limited physical contact. Most players have nothing to lose as they act out characters.

Fosters love: These role-play help invest the relationship for the partners to get to know each other. To play your partner's favorite character, you must know their preference.

Innovative: The sexual activity helps achieve sexual orgasm. It means that p realize their full potential to get results from imaginations.

Sex Games

Sex doesn't always have to be serious. Sex can be fun, too. In fact, laughter and a sense of play helps break the tension during new sexual experiences. Playing games and goofing around will bring you both out of your shell, allowing you to try new things and push each other's erotic boundaries comfortably.

Silent Sex

Sounds easy, right? Wrong. Try making love to your partner without making a sound. Do what you have to do: bite your lip, cover his mouth, and shove her face into a pillow…all is fair game.

To ramp up the stakes, whenever one of you makes a noise – the other person has to totally stop what they're doing.

You'll discover that when you're not allowed to express yourself verbally or vocally, you find another way to let that pleasure out through biting, squeezing, and desperately grabbing your partner to fuck you deeper.

Sex Dice

Your sexual experience is all up to fate with a roll of the dice.

Each set comes with two dice. One lists different activities like "lick", "tickle", "squeeze" and the other lists body parts like "nipples", "ass", "belly button".

This is a fun game to play with a glass of wine on the living room floor and watch where it leads.

Edging

When a vampire wants to turn human into a vampire, he must bite them without killing them. He must show extreme self-control and stop just before the human dies. You can think of Edging like this…without the whole death thing.

Edging is the act of coming so close to orgasm and then stopping. You repeat this over and over (3-4 times minimum) during the course of a few hours. When you finally let yourself or your partner cum…the orgasm will be one of the most intense you've ever had.

Make Bets with Dirty Wagers

Inject your sex life into everyday activities. When you're out and about, make sexy wagers on things like basketball games, whether or not it's going to rain, and how long it will take you to get home in this traffic.

The wages can be silly sexual things like "you have to lick peanut butter off of my nipples" or intense wagers like "you have to make me cum when we get home". You can one-up each other's wagers and set your own terms before you agree on the final bet.

To experiment with this challenge, pick a Sunday afternoon where the two of you spend the day together, taking turns setting wagers.

After the Sex Bucket List is complete, you might find yourselves carry this game on well into your future.

Porn Night

Take turns picking a porn- it doesn't matter the category. Start out with some categories neither of you watch on your own like MILF or Bondage to warm up- these are categories that you can both giggle about together and maybe get some new ideas. Go in with the mindset that this is going to be an entertaining activity together…while we all know that it's impossible not to get turned on during the process.

Eventually, start showing each other what you really like to watch…and see how long you can go without turning the night into your own porno.

The 10-Minute Rule

The dominant partner in this scenario sets a timer for 10 minutes. In those ten minutes, they tease their submissive partner relentlessly- nothing is off limits. The catch? The submissive partner is not allowed to touch the dominant partner until the timer goes off. But watch out, that timer will release a ravenous beast.

Strip Poker

Or Strip Chess. Or Strip Checkers. Or Strip Battle Ship. You can turn any game into a stripping game if you just believe in yourselves.

This kind of playful spirit brings out the flirt in both of you. The tease of watching clothes slowly coming off is wonderfully torturous. And that competitive edge will add a little spice to your dynamic.

If you want to step the game up one more level, you can make a rule that whomever is naked first receives a penalty of some slutty sex act or spankings

Weird Bonus Challenge: Tarzan and Jane

Bringing animal planet to the bedroom, things are about to get rough in this male pursuit/female resistance game. Secure ropes or ties to the corners of the bed. The goal is for Tarzan to wrestle Jane into submission, getting both of her hands and legs tightly secured. Jane's job is to resist.

While this 'Tarzan and Jane' might sound rapey, with a partner that you trust, this game can be so hot. It starts out playful and funny, then all of a sudden, your inner animal is unleashed, and you end up having the best rough and angry sex.

Finished the Challenge?

You dirty kids…

But hey, you're not done yet.

Now both of you need to scan through the past 100 sexual experiences and pick your top 5 sexual experiences.

Which naughty acts did you play over and over again in your head at work? Which one made you cum the hardest? Which one do you want to try again until you can perfect it?

Write them down and take turns reading them to each other, one by one.

Top 5 Sex Challenges

Her Top 5

1. ______________________________

2. ______________________________

3. ______________________________

4. ______________________________

5. ______________________________

His Top 5

1. ______________________________

2. ______________________________

3. ______________________________

4. ______________________________

5. ______________________________

Your New Naughty Challenge?

To explore the sexual experiences above, weaving them in your normal sex life…that is, if you can consider your sex life "normal" anymore.

Cut out 16 pieces of paper – 8 pieces each. Use each slip of paper to write your Top 5 sex challenges and 3 sex challenges that you'd like to try again.

Fold the papers and put them into a decorative bowl or a fish bowl. Twice a week for 8 weeks, you'll take turns picking a piece of paper out of the jar and acting out whatever is on that slip of paper.

Important: Designate two solid nights a week to do this. Write it on a calendar and do not skip it. Prioritize each other. Prioritize your sex life.

Advice for Beginners

Having sex for the first time can be an exciting and nervous experience full of anticipation. It involves a wide range of emotions. Once you become familiar with sex, even if on a basic level, you will begin to learn what brings you and your partner pleasure. It could be through a certain touch or sensation. Try to see how your lover reacts when you kiss or touch them in certain away. One of the most important ways to ease into sexual intimacy is through a gentle session of foreplay. This can be subtle, beginning with light kissing and touching, showing and exchanging signs of affection. During this phase, you may notice a decrease in anxiety and begin to experience signs of arousal. An erection is one of the initial signs in men, while women may feel their labia engorge and swell.

There may be slight wetness or moistening in the genital area, as well as heightened sensitivity to touch and sound. During this phase, the mutual attraction intensifies, which creates a transition to sex.

The Challenges of Sexual Education in Society

In many cultures and societies, sex education is considered taboo and avoided as much as possible. Even in countries where there is a more relaxed approach to the concept of sex and where it is introduced into the education system or tackled within the family, there still exists a gap between learning the fundamentals of biology and how to experience the pleasures of sexual activity. Sex education in most schools, for example, centers on the prevention of STIs (sexually transmitted infections), the concept of sexual arousal, and how the reproductive system works. In some progressive school systems, the curriculum has a broader spectrum of education to include all sexual orientations. These schools also have a more accepting approach to sexual and gender identity. However, there still exists a significant amount of resistance against a general openness to sexuality, and people are not generally taught how to enjoy and seek pleasure during sex.

Some family and marital arrangements have a heavy reliance on traditional practices that hold on to strict male and female roles. They place a more dominant role on men, with the expectation that women will always be sexually compliant and available even when there is no explicit consent. This power dynamic places men in a more commanding position where women's sexual needs and wants are suppressed.

On the other hand, men are expected to take on a traditional "leadership" role, which doesn't come with the goal of giving women pleasure or helping them achieve pleasure together as a couple. In relationships where there is both a lack of sexual education and mutual connection, sexual intimacy can be a major challenge, often done out of necessity and starting a family. Thus, it is less about pleasure and pleasing each other.

As some people break away from their traditional roles in marriage and intimate relationships, they realize there is much to learn from each other, especially on how to express their desires, bond with each other, and experience the joy of sex together.

While many people hold on to traditional views of marriage and sex, it is important to recognize the importance of learning the value of pleasure: how to please ourselves and our partners. This will only become easier for people once the stigma of sexual openness and communication fades away over time, allowing more discussion and direct communication about sex and how we can enjoy it.

Important Facts About Sex Everyone Should Know

Learning about sex goes beyond the basics of biology. It goes beyond responding to various cues and states of arousal. There are a lot of interesting facts to know about sex. If you are new to sex or less experienced, you will find that the early stages are a combination of learning from what you hear, read, and experience first-hand. If you are more knowledgeable than your partner, you can provide more guidance. However, care should always be taken so that both of you feel comfortable and willing to engage. The following important facts are vital and interesting, and they should be considered before you decide to engage with your partner.

1. Consent should be explicit.

When it comes to sex, a simple "Yes, I want to make love" is not always the way we consent or agree to have sex. When one partner initiates intimacy, the other may appear interested at first and then may hesitate later on. The reasons can vary, from changing their mind to simply not being interested in the moment. When there is the slightest doubt, it is important to establish whether consent is present, and make sure both of you are completely 100 percent willing without any reservations. There should be explicit consent, which means you and your partner should be fully in agreement and enthusiastic about it.

2. Sex is not going to be the same experience every time.

Some sessions will be ground breaking and exciting, leaving you wanting more. On other occasions, sex is less than thrilling and may not bring both or either partner to orgasm. This can be a result of various things — e.g., personal trauma in life, stress from family or work, or simply not feeling completely engaged or aroused in the experience. This is perfectly normal. It would be unusual to have ideal sex each and every time, as this is unrealistic. Do not expect this to happen always. It is important to be realistic, and accept the fact that, on some occasions, the spark may not be present. Be patient, and you will find that the best experiences will return again.

3. Long sessions of sex do not equate to better quality, and short, quick sex does not always have to be negative either.

It really depends on the couple and the circumstances. For example, in the morning, a quick session of early sex may be brief but highly passionate and satisfying. In fact, both lovers may be familiar enough with each other to bring about orgasm within a short time span, and then they go their separate ways for work and other daily activities. A longer session in a rushed morning would not accommodate their schedule. On the other hand, a slower, deeper intimacy in the evening hours can be satisfying in a completely different way, allowing both partners to experience more of each other.

4. Erection does not happen instantly every time, and when it does, it may occur when it is least expected.

A man may find himself with an erection in the morning during a shower or as he's getting ready for breakfast. A woman, on the other hand, may feel aroused during regular activities, such as attending a conference or running errands. When sex is initiated, it may take time to achieve an erection and natural arousal, even where both lovers are ready and excited to begin.

5. Lubrication is good for everyone.

It is wonderful how our bodies can create our own wetness, though it is best to add a bit of natural lubricant to your sexual encounter to avoid dryness and irritation later. There are various brands to choose from. You can also choose a variety of flavors and/or scents. There is also a choice between a more sensitive and natural fluid versus a more standard one. Take time to shop around with your partner to determine which one works best for both of you.

6. Moving from one position to another during sex is not always a simple task.

It mainly depends on your flexibility. Try new poses or positions, and switch them up every now and then. Some moves are going to take some practice, even exercise, to get them just right. Some positions may require your partner to lend you a hand, or you may need to help them steady their balance or ease slowly into a new pose. It may not look and feel glamorous, but it will be fun just the same!

7. Using protection is important, and knowing how to use it is vital.

Condoms are the most commonly used and preferred method of birth control and protection against STIs (sexually transmitted diseases). They are important early in the relationship. However, learning how to use a condom for the first time can be frustrating, and it often causes friction if not lubricated well. Condoms are not all created equally. Some brands may boast high sensitivity, while others are more durable and already lubricated, making it easier to put on. To avoid potential breakage and to ensure your experience is not spoiled, make sure you have a few condoms handy, just in case. Read the instructions carefully and take it slowly at first until you become used to the procedure. Remember that your partner can be helpful and give you much-needed support and assistance to get your session underway. There are creative and fun ways of putting on a condom, and this can fit easily into foreplay, making the experience much more enjoyable.

8. Sex is good for your health, and it is a form of exercise.

The more often you engage, the more calories you will burn. It is great for the heart and your body in general. Sex itself is a euphoric experience, causing a release of endorphins in the body, which reduces the likelihood of depression, anxiety, and other disorders. The frequency of sex varies from one couple to another, and while it is often more often at the beginning of the relationship, a routine will eventually become established. Even if you are engaging twice a week, there are fantastic benefits to your health and well-being.

9. Smoking can have a negative impact on your sex life.

Not only is smoking bad for your health, but it is also associated with lower rates of arousal and a decline in the strength of an erection. It can also affect endurance, making it difficult for the smoker to last longer in the bedroom, especially where there are respiratory conditions involved. If you currently smoke, consider quitting or taking steps to decrease the amount you use, as this will make a major improvement over time.

10. Orgasm is not going to happen every time you have sex.

You can have a hot and passionate session with your partner and not achieve a climax. Likewise, your partner can experience the same; it happens for both men and women. It can cause feelings of disappointment and insecurity. It is normal for this to occur sometimes, even between health-loving couples.

11. The more you communicate, the better your sex life will be.

Many people avoid talking about certain topics, including sex and intimacy. When communication breaks down, it can lead to a lot of misunderstandings, hurt, and avoidance. Intimacy can eventually break down until it reaches the point where it is no longer a part of a couple's life. Once this happens, it can lead to marital or relationship breakdown as well. Keeping the conversation alive is the best way to enjoy all that your relationship can provide.

There are many other facts about sex that you can learn in a variety of ways. One of the best ways to get familiar with your body and to engage with your partner is through open dialogue and discussion about a variety of concerns, including your fantasies and desires (Gordon, 2018).

Five Uncommon Facts That Can Improve Your Sex Life

Getting comfortable with your partner will not only help improve your sex life but will also give you the confidence to ask questions and better understand how you can mutually pleasure each other. Exploring various techniques and ideas and having openness to doing so has a major impact on the success of your love life and how well it will develop over time. Couples who explore and communicate about sex without reservation tend to lead healthier, happier lives in general, not just in the bedroom.

There are a few unexpected ideas and facts that make a positive impact on your sex life. Some of these facts dispel myths about sex, giving us a different perspective on how to enjoy our love life. They also create a healthy outlook about sex and how we engage with our partner and ourselves.

1. The most sexual part of our body is our brain.

The onset of arousal and the creation of sexual fantasies begin here. It is our mind that plays the most significant role in how we experience lovemaking and how we connect with our partner. Our perception (the signals our body and mind process and send throughout our body during foreplay and sex) sets the stage for a spectacular series of sensations. Alternatively, when our thoughts or impressions about a specific scenario are negative, it affects our body's response. For example, if we feel hesitant about pursuing a specific technique with our partner or lack trust in them for some reason, even the usual pleasurable event of lovemaking can be unenjoyable. This is because your mind isn't completely involved or relaxed for the experience. When we feel connected in mind and body, sex only gets better over time.

2. Women only orgasm 20 percent of the time during sex.

This is usually because some men believe women can achieve climax with vaginal sex alone, whereas this is not often the case. In fact, most women need clitoral stimulation or oral sex to bring themselves to orgasm. In some positions, it is possible for both men and women to reach orgasm together, which can be incredibly pleasurable, though it can also take practice and time to achieve. It is also advantageous for couples to explore various forms of arousal, as well as positions that include oral sex. This will greatly increase the chances of orgasm for women and can help men as well.

3. Men also fake orgasms.

Women often admit to this, though men have been found to do this as well and often for the same reason: they want to please their partner or give the impression that they have been adequately satisfied. This may be a way for men to assure their partner that they are able to reach orgasm quickly and to convey confidence. For women, there are several reasons. Like men, they want to show their satisfaction or at least convince their partner of it. Faking an orgasm gives the other person the satisfaction of being able to bring their partner to climax and, therefore, boosts their ego or confidence. The problem with this technique is dishonesty. Faking an experience you should want to enjoy is not giving you any real pleasure, while at the same time, it gives your partner the wrong impression of what works for you.

4. Headaches and pain can often disappear or subside during sex.

The popular excuse for declining sex, "Not tonight, I have a headache," is usually joked about as a means to avoid intimacy or skip sex. In reality, such an excuse could mean something more, especially if it is a recurring phrase (or something similar). There may be a hidden discomfort associated with sex that your partner may not feel like explaining, though they may be more direct and open with patience and understanding. It is important to communicate to find out the real reasons for lack of intimacy and to gently approach the topic so as not to push or pressure your partner to explain everything, especially if

there is (or are) reason(s) why they may not feel up to it
(Hubby, 2017).

5. Many women masturbate, though they tend not to discuss it
as freely or widely as men, mostly due to societal expectations
and ideals.

Even where women have made great strides forward in
freedom, including sexual expression and liberation, there are
still items considered less favorable when broached by a woman
than a man. Masturbation is one of these topics, as well as sex
in general. However, this is changing, and women are becoming
more vocal and expressive than ever. Masturbation, or self-
pleasure, should never be a source of shame, whether you enjoy
it for yourself or mutually with your partner (Carson, 2017).

Sex Positions for Beginners

It is important to understand that while some positions may be
great for you your partner may not love them. So, trying
different things and having an Arsenal of different sex positions
to try is advantageous in having excellent sexual sessions. Here

again, you need to be open to experimentation. Trying out different positions can lead you to a whole new world of ecstasy that you have never experienced.

Let's start out by looking at some of the most basic sex positions that can be accomplished while laying down and how to actually make them happen. However, they may surprise you once you actually give them a try. So, don't feel as if the basics aren't good enough as often times they absolutely are.

The first position that we would like to look at is the face to face position. To accomplish this both parties will be laying on their sides. You'll be facing each other. The female will be slightly higher on the bed than her male counterpart. This is so that her hips are above his. One of her legs will wrap around the top of him and the other one should be laid down straight. Sometimes this can feel a bit awkward but with practice, it feels truly great.

This is a fantastic position for beginners because it helps you to gain comfort with your partner. It is a very intimate position that will allow deeper levels of penetration. The closeness of this position also helps both to relax and enjoy the experience.

We have one of the most common positions, missionary style. This is done by the female lying flat on her back and the male on top of her. The female's legs can be in a variety of different positions. Sometimes, she will lay them down flat on the bed while other times she may wrap them around her partner's waist. This simply comes down to what is most comfortable. Other people prefer to have their knees bent so that their feet are flat on the bed and their knees are facing the ceiling.

Missionary position is basic but essential for beginners. It is one of our go-to moves. It allows for different positioning which can help both parties achieve orgasm more easily. It tends to be very comfortable for both the man and the woman. You will be facing each other, and this will allow you to focus on the level of intimacy that you are exuding. Additionally, it will make it easy to communicate what your needs are if the position needs to change slightly.

Spooning is another basic position that offers a great deal of satisfaction for both parties. To accomplish this, you will lay in the spoon position. The female's hips should be above her partners. The Top leg will need to be lifted slightly so that penetration can occur. Sometimes this feels a bit awkward and you may need to adjust your positioning to find a good level of comfort.

This position is fantastic for beginners because it allows for stimulation to the females G-spot quite easily. It can be very comfortable once you find the right fit. You won't have to worry about doing a whole lot of work but both parties will be able to move fairly easily. The involvement of both people is appreciated on both sides and it is likely that you will fall in love with this basic position.

Now that we have looked at some awesome positions that you can use while laying down will move on to some sitting positions. Sitting positions can allow for deeper levels of penetration which can, in turn, offer higher levels of stimulation for both parties. Sitting positions are usually very easy to achieve and are a natural go-to for couples that are inexperienced, as well as, experienced.

The first position that we are going to discuss is a combination of a lying down and sitting position. This position is most commonly referred to as the cowgirl style. To accomplish it, the male will lay flat on his back with his legs stretched out in front of him. The woman will climb on Top and straddle him. How she chooses to position her legs should be in whatever position is the most comfortable. From here she will have the ability to take control and ride her male counterpart.

Beginners love this position because it is easy to accomplish. It is important to note that if the female puts her feet flat on the bed with her knees facing the ceiling or the wall it will be a bit difficult to do this for very long. The motion will be difficult on her thigh muscles. However, this can be combated by putting one shin down on the bed and leaving the other in the upward position. It provides great leverage and an excellent level of penetration. Additionally, it will allow the woman to ride the man's penis in a way that stimulates her G-spot.

You can modify this position in a variety of different ways. To make it a true sitting position you simply need to change the position of the man. Rather than him lying on his back have him sit with his back leaning against a solid surface. He can bend his knees or leave them straight just depending on what feels best for both parties. From there the female is going to do the exact same thing as stated above.

It is important to note that some women will find this position to be intimidating if they're lacking in, experience. This is due to the fact that they are extremely exposed. However, as long as you have an intimate and trusting connection with your partner it is definitely worth giving this position a try. It can lead to excellent levels of stimulation an ecstasy.

You can alter the cowgirl into another position by simply turning the female around. This is referred to as a reversed cowgirl. It provides a different stimulation to both the man and the woman. This is due to the fact that the underside of the man's penis will now be rubbing the front wall of the woman's vagina. This type of stimulation can be fantastic for reaching climax and providing mind-blowing orgasms.

Now we're going to move on to a couple of basic kneeling positions that you can easily enter into during sexual encounters. Kneeling positions can be truly amazing for both parties. This is due to the fact that you tend to have a good amount of movement and deeper levels of penetration in positions where one or both parties are kneeling.

The first position that we want to look at is the doggie style. This is one of the most popular positions for inexperienced, as well as, experienced people. Many find that this is one of their favorite positions because of the level of penetration and movement that can be experienced. In addition, men tend to like the view of their ladies from behind.

To accomplish the doggie style position is fairly simple. The woman will need to be on her hands and knees or on her forearms and knees. The man will approach her from behind. Her knees should be about shoulder-width apart so that her man can kneel between them. He will then enter her from behind. More often than not the man will hold on to the woman's hips which will give him some control over the speed and power of his thrust. However, this position is also good if the woman wants to take control.

There are different variations of the doggie style position. Sometimes, the woman will lay flat on her stomach and the man will kneel over top of her. This can be a bit more challenging than a basic doggie style position, but it is also very exciting. It will make the female feel tighter around her man's member and heighten the level of pleasure that both parties experience.

Now we move on to some basic standing positions. There are many variations of standing positions that are very easy to accomplish. However, you need to be aware that some standing positions are very difficult to participate in for long periods of time. Don't get discouraged if you can't participate in standing positions for a long time, just keep at it and it will get easier the more experienced you are.

The first position we are going to look at is a combination of standing and kneeling positions. In this position, the woman will kneel on the bad like she would in a doggie style position. The difference is the man will be standing. He will approach the woman from behind and place his legs between hers. This will give him excellent leverage. He will also be able to grab her by the hips and control the speed and thrust at which intercourse is performed.

This position is extremely easy to accomplish and exceptionally pleasurable for both parties. He will be able to play with depth to tease her and truly provide her with a variety of sensations. More than likely both parties will be able to participate in this position for a decent amount of time as it is not physically demanding.

Another standing position that is great well require the use of a chair. Both parties will be standing. The woman will face forward and lean over bracing herself on the chair. She will spread her legs so that they are shoulder with apart. It is important to note that if you are dealing with a partner who is much taller or shorter than you, you may need to stand up on your toes or kneel slightly. The man will then approach her from behind with his legs between hers wow he enters her. This position can be a little bit tired so, if you can't do it for very long don't get discouraged.

It is important to note that not everybody will be able to accomplish it. There are a couple of variations but to accomplish this position the woman will have her back against the wall. You will be face to face with your partner. She will want to raise one or both of her legs so that they are around her partner's waist. The man will then position himself to be able to penetrate her. It will require a decent amount of strength from the man as he will be supporting quite uh a lot of the woman's weight. This is especially true if she is intending unwrapping both legs around his waist. This position provides an insane level of penetration. There will not be a ton of movement, but the sensations can allow both parties to reach orgasm quite easily.

Once you have experimented with these sex positions, you'll be able to move into other ones. Understand that there are hundreds of different positions that you can try out. We have only given you the tip of the iceberg. There are many other basic positions that are easy to accomplish. In addition, there are more advanced ones that will take some practice. When you're comfortable with your sexual partner experimenting with sex positions becomes extremely easy. Additionally, it helps to heighten the experience and keep things interesting if you are in a long-term relationship.

How to Use Your Hands

How you make your sex drive determines whether your partner enjoys sex. Partners find it hard to keep up with the poor performance of their partners in bed. Various factors, such as stress, make partners hard to turn on. As a result, couples lose their meaning and value in intercourse, making it happen rarely enjoyable. Therefore, you should learn how to spice things up and create an intimate and relaxing environment. With essential tools, there are ways you could transition your partner from being stressed to blissed. It is possible to use your readily available hands to achieve great sexual satisfaction for you and your partner. However, you should understand how to do it to avoid backlash and counter-productivity. The following are ways you could apply your hands and create wild sensation to your partner.

1. ***Stimulate Your Partner:*** The soft touches that you make to your partner mean a lot to them, for it shows connectivity as well as boosting their sexual consciousness. You should ensure that your partner feels you as you caress them and make sensitive touches that arouse them sexually. Your hands are a powerful tool that could turn your partner on if done appropriately and suggestively. The stimulation could be done before, during, and after sexual intercourse as long as it happens with moderation. If your partner has the body covered most of the time, they will enjoy it when hands reach the places that are usually covered.

2. ***Guidance:*** Most of the sex positions involve partners lying on the bed or being in a position that leaves only the hands free. They provide an ample opportunity for you to communicate with your partner. Your hands are the best tools to guide your partner in areas

that are most stimulating and how to touch them.
Men use their hands to hold the woman's head as
they receive oral to guide them on the depth and pace.
Similarly, you may use your hand to keep your
partner's head as you kiss. This way, you are sure to
get the best out of it.

3. **Self-stimulation:** It is yet another way to make
    yourself appreciative and making fun of the moment.
    Sexual stimulation is not only achieved by the touch
    of your partners but also your contact. You could use
    your hands to stimulate your body by working on the
    nipples or the clitoris. Self-stimulation is regarded as
    accurate for you to know the parts that cause much
    stimulation as well as how you should caress them.
    Similarly, you are aware of the limitation to that
    stimulation as opposed to external stimulation which
    cannot tell when you have enough of it. Self-
    Stimulation makes it possible to reach spots that your
    partner cannot primarily in a complicated position.

4. **Achieve orgasm:** It has become common among

couples to use their hands to achieve inevitable orgasm. Most couples find the hands so sensitive to their genitals that they must be used to help the orgasm. Your soft hand could turn and reach hidden spots in your partner's genitals are if only they guide you on the stimulation they need. You could use your fingers to penetrate the vagina and reach the G spot, which could turn the woman wild and wanting. The same mechanism could be applied in the case of anal sex to stimulate the nerve endings.

5. ***Control:*** Much of these controls occurs during sexual intercourse. It is common in the cowgirl, missionary, and doggy sex positions. As a dominant partner in these positions, you could use your hands to control the movement of your partner as well as bringing them closer to the action. Besides, your hands are vital in controlling the depth and pace of the penetration for a best intimate session. In cowgirl, you make her move horizontally helps control your point of ejaculation while enhancing the contact of your pelvis with that of the clitoris. You could also change the partner's posture using your hands for a more

pleasuring sexual act. Women like to wrap their sides around the man's waist to enhance the pace and help them make a deep penetration.

6. ***Utilizing Sex Toys:*** You would not want to live all your sex life without having to try sex toys. Most probably, you have already tried a number of them and realized the pleasure associated with them. There are different types of sex toys, and most have various forms of application, even though they may appear identical. Besides, you should perfect on the usage of each sex toy before trying it on your partner to avoid mess and embarrassment. Your hands are then the essential tools when it comes to how effective a sex toy is. You should have a firm grip on the object to ensure that it meets its desired objectives. During sexual intercourse, you should involve sex toys, especially for foreplay and maintenance of sexual stimulation. Your hands should act as the support and director of the toy as it is busy stimulates the sensitive parts of your partner.

7. ***Demonstration:*** At times, partners do not get what they want due to a lack of providing feedback. You should be free to each other on what works best for you and what does not. If your partner does not get what you are asking for, you could use your own hands to show them what they should do to impress you sexually. It includes touching your sensitive parts that your partner may be missing or showing them the pace with which to land on them. You could perform a session they watch to understand what they need to correct and what to expect in every move they make. For instance, you could masturbate to show your partner how you want them to or how easy it is for you to reach orgasm.

8. ***Support:*** Most sex positions require couples to be in postures that require them to use hands for support. These are positions that would be suitable for physically fit couples. For instance, the missionary position requires the man to use his hands for help as he penetrates the partner. Numerous variants of sex positions leave only the hands suspended with

the other part of the body fixed in a non-supportive place. Partners may also use their hands as pillows to raise their heads or buttock for clear vision or penetration. The support that your hands provide makes you comfortable while enhancing the strength, depth, and pace of the penetration. In the 69 positions, the hand's aid in ensuring that the genitals are easily accessible and serviceable. The support provided in the missionary position ensures that the man focuses on stimulation penetration.

You should not let your sex life to lose value and test due to inefficiency caused by how you go down on your partner. Take a step of reshaping your sex life by incorporating additional sexual moves and techniques. These ideas will help shape your relationship as you explore some of the insights provided. They will also help you learn more about your partner and understand what works best for them.

Have Fun and Play Dirty

Aside from a penis, a tongue, or fingers, a vibrator can be a woman's best friend. If you're a woman that doesn't have a vibrator (you poor, deprived thing!), you might want to consider getting one. Not only is it a great masturbation tool and a fine stress reliever, but it's also a wonderful way to share a sexual experience with your partner. Vibrators come in a variety of different shapes, sizes, styles, etc. You can get the old school, white plastic model, or you can go for the ultra-realistic looking dildo in the shape and size of your favorite male porn star.

How to get the best out of it

Some people view sex toys as something that is for those who have wild kinks or those who cannot perform without assistance of some sort. In reality, though, sex toys are designed to increase and enhance pleasure for anyone. By using sex toys, you do not have to engage in anything wild or anything that you are uncomfortable with. You are also not admitting that you have a sexual problem by using a sex toy.

One of the ways in which sex toys can improve your sex life is that they allow you to focus on one area of the body while the sex toy takes care of pleasure in another. For example, a sex toy that is designed to pleasure a woman's clitoris will do so while you can focus on her nipples or her vagina.

Finding the right toy

In order to choose the right sex toy for yourself, there are a couple of questions that you would need to answer first.

· Is this toy to be used alone during masturbation?

· Is it to be used with a partner?

· Is it to be used with multiple partners?

· Is it to be used for all of the above or two of the above?

· Do you want it to have a vibrating function?

· An insertion function?

· Will you use it anally?

· Vaginally?

· Both?

· Do you want it to be customizable (depending on your mood or the partner you are with)?

Once you establish this, you will be able to narrow down your search. Answering all of these questions will help you to determine which type of sex toy is right for you (and your partner).

Sex position and sex toys

Once you've got your first four sex toys ready, it's time to combine this with some sex positions and begin exploring just how much pleasure the introduction of something new can bring. Of course, you can start getting a little more adventurous later once both partners are comfortable with the idea of using these toys in the bedroom. Until then, these positions will serve as a good first step to test the waters:

The Missionary with Vibrator

Time to get back to basics once more as you slowly familiarize each other with the use of these sex toys. The woman will be lying down on her back on the bed, relaxed and ready. The man starts off slow and gentle, locating her clitoris with his fingers. Turn the vibrator on a low buzz, slowly bring it between her legs and place it so that it lightly touches her clitoris. The man then watches her facial expressions change as he tries varying amounts of pressure and speed settings of the vibrator.

Occasionally take her by surprise by slipping a finger inside her vagina and find her G-spot while the vibrator is still going. Listen to her moans of desire for your cues to help her reach intense levels of pleasure. Adjust the speed when you're ready, increasing the speed as the woman gets wetter and wetter.

Doggy Style with The Strap-On

The Doggy position, when combined with a strap-on creates a mecca of pleasure. This time, however, it is the man who is going to be in the Doggy position while the woman wears the strap on and do what you normally would do in this position. Be careful when playing with the man's anus, and don't forget to use lots of lube for this one.

Seated Sex Position with the Vibrating Cock Ring

With the Cock Ring positioned at the base of the man's penis, vibrating and ready, the man sits in a chair while the woman sits on his lap, facing him with her legs around his waist and behind you. Have her stand up slightly, so she is hovering before she lowers herself onto the vibrating penis. Work together to move her body up and down on your penis. She can rotate her hips slightly backward, and the vibrating ring should stimulate her clitoris. The vibration of the ring will give her intense pleasure, and this position is ideal for a great male orgasm and a great female orgasm too.

Masturbation

Man's secret pleasure point

Male masturbation is described as the act of a man pleasuring himself by either touching or stimulating his penis, nipples, testicles, and other erogenous zones in his body. These self-pleasuring techniques usually carry on to the point of ejaculation or orgasm, and it is done purely to satisfy his sexual pleasure. This can be done either solo or when you're in private or as part of the foreplay leading up to sex with their partner, although most of the time, masturbation typically happens when the man is alone. As a man, masturbation can help you deal with anxieties, understand your sexual preferences, your body, improve your endurance during sex and generally keeps you happy.

Woman's secret pleasure point

Masturbation can be just as life-changing for a woman's sex life as it can be for a man. Many women struggle with body issues and poor self-image, but masturbation is a way of overcoming that and learning to love your body as it is. When you know how to pleasure yourself, it makes it easier to guide your partner about what they need to go to take your orgasms to the next level. Self-love is important for a woman because it can deeply affect your intimacy with your partner when you're not comfortable in your own skin. If you haven't spent a lot of time pleasuring yourself before this, it's never too late to start.

First, get to know your body better by holding a mirror between your legs to see what your partner sees when they are touching you or giving you oral sex. Take a good look at what you look like down there. This is you. This is your body. Now, start to feel around a little bit, massaging your vulva and locating your clitoris. Play around the area and observe the way your body responds to the touch. Some areas will feel oh so good while others will feel very, VERY good. You want to keep the sensation going on the "very good" areas.

Hand tricks to give extreme pleasure

Masturbation is often thought of as a solo act, but it could be surprisingly pleasurable to do this with your partner. Masturbation is an intimate thing and sharing this moment with someone you care about can bring you closer together as a couple. Mutual masturbation can be an incredible moment shared between you and your partner. For the man, watching his partner masturbate is probably high on his sexual wish list. It may not be as high on the list for the woman, but you may be surprised at how arousing it could be. As a bonus, you may each learn something new about your partner's arousal process. Some women may never even have seen a man ejaculate in real life other than is watched in porn films. Men, ejaculating in front of your partner is a very intimate act, and surprisingly enough, many women find it arousing not only physically but mentally and emotionally.

Face-to-Face

This position can be pulled off in a few ways, depending on how you and your partner like to do it. Begin by lying down on your side, facing your partner, and gazing into their eyes. The closer you are, the greater the intimacy and intensity of the moment. Touch yourself the way you would if you were masturbating alone and watch your partner's face start to change as they pleasure themselves too. It's a great time to throw in some dirty talk here. Keep this going until you both climaxes, perhaps even try attempting to orgasm at the same time.

Don't Ask

Instead of asking for sex, show your partner that you're in the mood instead. This tip works best for women, and without saying a word, position yourself provocatively comfortably and make sure he's got a good view. Place two fingers in an inverted V straddling your clitoris. This hand position is good for encouraging your orgasm. Throw yourself into your masturbation session with abandon and watch his face start to change as continues watching you pleasure yourself.

Stimulating His Testicles

This secret is key to giving your man some of the best orgasms of his life. This secret is in the testicles and knowing how to use them as a secret weapon of pleasure. Cup your partner's testicles gently and begin stroking them softly. Hold them and very lightly pull them towards you (be gentle here because his testicles will be sensitive to your touch). To double the pleasure, give him fellatio while you do this, it's going to drive him crazy as the stimulation of both his penis and his balls at the same time will make it hard for him not to finish right then and there. The warmth and moisture of your mouth around his penis, along with his testicles being gently rubbed will lead straight to orgasmic bliss.

Spice it up with dirty talks

What to say and when

That sometimes difficult, but always necessary sex conversation is what we are going, to begin with. This conversation can be difficult to work up to, especially if you have not had many conversations like this outside of dirty talk in the bedroom. What I'm talking about is an adult conversation where you ask them what they want, what they need, and what they like and dislike. This conversation is one that should happen in every relationship when you first begin a sexual relationship and should be revisited over and over again throughout the course of your relationship, but it is never too late to have this conversation for the first time.

Communication outside the Bedroom

The best way to communicate outside the bedroom is to have a conversation at a time when you are both unaroused, and your feelings won't be clouded by sexual frustration. If, after talking about this, you are both so horny that you go and jump on each other in the bedroom, that's fine, but begin this conversation in a different time and place so that it can be a serious dialogue about both of your needs.

Communication During Sex

During sex is an important time to check in with your partner to see how she is feeling, what she is liking, and what she wants more of. This is also a time where you can tell her what you like and what you want more of. While you are having sex, it is easiest to communicate using dirty talk so that you don't ruin the mood by coming off too serious or too concerned. In order to properly communicate while also playing into the mood of the moment, you can do so in a sexy way, using sexy language. You should tell each other what you like by saying, "oh yes, I like that" or "I like when you touch me like that" This lets the person know to do more of the same because this is what will get you to orgasm. If your girl seems like she is really enjoying what you are doing, don't change it up, keep doing the same. With a woman, if you find that thing she likes- don't give it up! It may be hard for you both to find the spot she likes and the way she likes it, so if she is getting hot and bothered by the way you are touching her, keep it up. You can ask her to let you know when she likes the way you are touching her and let her know that this will help you to give her great orgasms.

Communication After Sex

Next time you have sensual pillow talk, ask them what their favorite part was. Ask her what she liked and what you did that was different than before. You can open up this dialogue by telling her how sexy you thought she was or how you liked it when she did a certain thing to your penis. After sex is a good time for this because it is fresh in your minds and you can revisit it together while you both still remember exactly what you did to each other.

Periods and Sex

Women get their menstrual period during their reproductive years. It is at this time that they or their partner wonder whether it is safe to have sex. The fact that the vagina has to be covered with a tampon to absorb the blood complicates the situation. If you find yourself in this situation, it is advisable to consult your partner and find the best ways to meet your sexual desires during the periods. Sex during periods is considered safe, and partners should explore the various means to achieve intimacy.

Moreover, they should understand that at times the intercourse may get messy if you fail to adhere to considerations. There are numerous benefits associated with sex during periods, especially if done through the most appropriate sex positions. However, you must make the following considerations to enjoy sex during periods.

Considerations When Having Sex During Periods

1. *Consult*: As always, it is crucial to make the necessary consultation as you indulge in what your partner may find weird or uncomfortable. You should help them understand all aspects of the activity, as well as the precautions that you will put in place. Both partners should be willing to have sex during periods to get the best out of it.

2. *Plan*: Sex during periods requires planning, as you may need additional equipment to put away the mess.

You and your partner should be comfortable with the place and manner in which the activity will take place.

3. *Make preferences*: As equals in the relationship, you should allow your partner to choose what they prefer while planning to have sex. Women should advise their men on when it is best to have sex during the period as they know when they experience lighter flows of blood.

4. *Foreplay*: You should come up with the best type of foreplay that matches the situation. In this case, you should avoid messy foreplay and opt for an alternative. For instance, the 69 position foreplay would not be advisable during periods as it would expose your mouth to the menstrual blood and possibly infections.

5. *Tampon*: Remember to remove the tampon before engaging in active sex to enhance penetration and intimacy. Besides, the failure to remove the tampon may result in medical emergencies as it may get stuck

in the vagina requiring medical expertise to remove it.

6. ***Towels:*** Ensure that you prepare the platform where the activity will happen and place the necessary equipment at your convenience. Similarly, you may need to lay a dark-colored towel on the bed as it may play a significant role in absorbing any leakages. It would avoid making the bed messy from menstrual blood.

7. ***Protection:*** It is advisable to use a latex condom when penetrating during periods. It would help avoid numerous irregularities that may arise as a result of unprotected sex. It includes the contraction of STIs as well as limiting the amount of blood that flows out of the vagina.

8. ***Position:*** There are specific positions to practice when having sex during periods to enhance penetration and prevent excess blood flow from the vagina. Therefore, you should come up with considerate

positions that would be appropriate for both partners and make the activity as safe as possible.

9. ***Pregnancy:*** There is a misconception that women cannot conceive when they have sex during their periods. This misconception has brought trouble to families after thinking that they practice safe sex, but their pregnancy results test positive. It is worth noting that ovulation may overlap with periods making it possible to conceive at this time. Similarly, the sperms could remain active in the oviduct up to five days after intercourse. Therefore, if the periods ended within the timeframe, it is most likely that the woman will conceive. For this reason, you should take the appropriate measures, such as using a condom to avoid unwanted pregnancies.

Pros of Sex during Periods

Relieves cramps: When a woman experiences orgasm during her periods, she releases hormones that relieve cramps. It eases the difficulty and pain that they experience during their periods, making it essential for sexual stimulation.

Shortens periods: During sexual stimulation, the uterus walls make a contraction that releases more blood. As a result, the woman experiences an increased amount of blood that flows out of the vagina. It also increases the rate at which the blood flows out. Consequently, the uterus is quickly emptied, shortening the time required for the periods and easing the anxiety associated with it.

Increased sex drive: It is common for women to have hormonal imbalance during their periods. It would be advisable to engage in sexual activities to alter the imbalance and enhance stimulation that leads to a consistent sex drive. This aspect would help reverse the notion of low sex drive during periods.

Lubrication: Sexual intercourse needs to be lubricated to avoid fractures and injuries. That is why both partners produce sexual fluids that facilitate penetration and thrusting. Menstrual blood offers additional lubrication during sex, making it safe and enjoyable.

Anti-depressant: Women may be depressed whenever they experience their periods either due to cramps or inability to please their partner sexually. However, the discovery that sex is possible even during periods would help them have peace of mind as they have their side effects wiped out.

STIs: Practicing unprotected sex during periods could lead to sexually transmitted Infections that could be a health concern for both partners. Being exposed to the woman's blood may facilitate the spread of hepatitis B, Gonorrhea, or HIV. Similarly, women could contract these infections if exposed to sexual fluids from the man.

Unwanted Pregnancy: Couples may be unaware of the possibility of a pregnancy in case the man ejaculates. It mostly happens with unprotected sex, where there is a high chance of conceiving for the ovulation that may overlap with periods. The sperms may also be preserved in the production duct and fertilize after the period's end.

Limited Sex Position: Some positions could not work for you, especially if the woman is having her periods. There are suitable positions that would work best for such a condition to avoid mess and disappointments. For instance, there are variations of the cowgirl that would let out an excessive amount of blood. It is not what you should choose to practice if you want an enjoyable intimate session with your partner.

Best Sex Positions during Periods

1. ***Non-Penetrative:*** You could decide to practice non-penetrative sex if your partner is on her periods. This form of sex involves a stimulating sex session that would lead to orgasm and possibly ejaculation. With this form, you do not have to worry about the safety measures and considerations for sex during periods.

2. ***Anal:*** It is a form of sex that involves penetrating the anus. It excludes the participation of the vagina and would still lead to sexual stimulation and orgasm. With this form of sex, the woman could be having her

tampon on as the man makes moves on the anus.

3. ***Shower Sex:*** As the name suggests, the activity is performed in a running shower where the water above cleans the mess quickly and frequently. It ensures that no blood stick son the body making it fun and intimate.

4. ***Doggy:*** As the woman bends over, she aims to oppose the force of gravity that would let excess blood out. The position allows the man to have excellent access to the G spot while experiencing little or no blood marks.

5. ***Missionary:*** The positions variants are perfect for sex during periods. The woman may decide to put her feet on the man's shoulders as she lies on a flat platform. The position creates an uphill for the flowing blood as well as providing excellent clit stimulation from the man o top.

Sex in Pregnancy

Pregnancy is the ultimate result for couples who had plenty of bedroom sessions. The sessions may have been a result of the urge to conceive and make a family. Most partners lose interest in sex after designing or if their partners conceive. If you suffer from the same condition, you should take measures to ensure that you do not lose interest in intimacy due to a short term condition. You may have difficulties expressing your feelings for each other due to concerns over pregnancy. It is safe to have sex during pregnancy and may be beneficial for you and the unborn. It is worth noting that there is a need to be cautious when having sex in at this time to ensure that you do not cause trouble. For that reason, you should make the following considerations for a safe and intimate session during pregnancy.

Considerations for Sex in Pregnancy

Discuss: It is an essential aspect of sex during pregnancy as the partners should be comfortable and relaxed for an intimate session. The discussion should involve the positions that you will incorporate throughout the session, as well as the pace and depth of penetration.

Besides, you should get a doctor's approval after doing the necessary check-ups that will give the go-ahead or make reservations.

Limitations: You should also understand the barriers that are associated with sex during pregnancy. They include keeping a low paced performance and making the session as intimate and straightforward as possible. Besides, other limitations should be observed to ensure that you do not affect the pregnancy and specifically the unborn baby. It includes avoiding combining anal sex and vaginal sex, as it may lead to the transfer of bacteria.

Records: While having sex during pregnancy, you should ensure that it does not bring complications to the woman or the unborn baby. Avoid engaging in this form of sex if your partner has a history of miscarriage.

History: You must have known your partner if she is pregnant for you. For that reason, you should ensure that the activity does not affect the timing of her labor. Similarly, you should look out for the history of membrane eruption that is mostly associated with deep penetration and hard-hitting. Membrane eruption is as a result of leakages of the amniotic fluid that acts as a protector from external factors.

Cervix: You need to take your partner for a thorough check-up of the cervix to ensure that it is in the perfect condition that makes it right for sex. Ignoring this consideration may lead to other severe conditions that would require special attention from medical experts.

Positions: The big bump in pregnancy may act as a facilitator or an obstruction during sex. Therefore, you should opt for flexible positions that make it easy for both of you. The side by side rear entry position acts as a perfect example of positions that would be easy and sexually stimulating.

Make Necessary Reports: You should check on your partner every time you have sex to ensure that there are no abnormalities or straining. Make appropriate reports to the doctor if you detect problems such as pain or discharge during sex. These discharges may include blood, which is a clear indication of a severe malfunction. If any of these problems in observed, you should leave the sexual activity and ensure that you take necessary actions to inhibit them.

Maintain Intimacy: Regardless of the stage of pregnancy, you should maintain intimate sessions before, during, and after pregnancy. It will make it easier to resume positions even after your partner delivers.

Failure to maintain intimacy after your partner conceives may lower her self-esteem and eventually lose interest in future sex. Consequently, you would require a desperate measure to rejuvenate the mood or miss it altogether.

Pros of Sex in Pregnancy

1. ***Eases labor.*** Frequent sex sessions make it easy for the woman to give birth and recover. The contraction of muscles experienced during sex aids in strengthening the pelvic muscles. As a result, the vagina easily opens up while resuming its previous state due to the flexibility of muscles.

2. ***Fewer breaks:*** The contractions cause muscle movements to make it easy for the vagina to hold any discharge that is associated with pregnancy. As a result, the woman can hold for long, thus requiring less time for making bathroom breaks.

3. ***Prevention:*** Engaging in sex while pregnant is beneficial for it incorporates nutrients from the sperms that aid in the growth of the unborn and the well-being of the woman. The proteins found in sperms offers nutrients that help prevent pre-eclampsia.

4. ***Controls Blood Pressure:*** Sex controls your blood pressure when you are pregnant. The activity itself acts as an exercise that aids in blood circulation throughout the body, strengthening your immune system and respiration. These are essential aspects that determine your health and that of the unborn.

5. ***Boosts mood:*** It is common to experience mood swings, especially when you are pregnant. The condition worse if your partner shows no sexual expression. For that reason, you should engage in frequent sex to maintain orgasm remain focused. Orgasm induces the circulation of blood in your pelvis, which is vital for the health of your uterus and vagina. The ripened pelvis makes it right to prepare for labor and safe delivery.

6. ***Improves Self-Esteem:*** Pregnancy comes with its effects on how you perceive yourself. The biological processes that take place during this time affect the hormonal balance hence the lowering of self-esteem.

However, your partner's sexual stimulation and caressing revamp your self-confidence as you feel treasured and adored regardless of the condition.

7. ***Reduces Stress***: The loneliness associated with pregnancy nay make a woman indulges in self-examination and worries about the unborn. The most common results are depression and stress, which could reduce through companionship and intimacy. By caring for your pregnant partner and giving her the best sexual stimulation, you reduce her stress and refresh her mind.

8. ***Nurtures Your Relationship***: Sex during pregnancy jakes it clear that you love your partner unconditionally. They feel endowed and appreciated knowing that they hold a precious gift in them. Finding time to connect with your partner during pregnancy boost a mutual connection which soars even after conception.

1. ***Premature Labor:*** There have been cases of premature labor in couples who engage in sex during pregnancy. The cases are high, especially if the pregnancy is in the third trimester. For this reason, you should consult your doctor before engaging in sex at this period.

2. ***Vaginal Bleeding:*** The sensitivity of the pelvis makes it prone to injury, especially if the man makes a deep penetration or hits it hard. There may be excessive bleeding putting the woman at risk of low blood count, which is a severe condition in pregnancy.

3. ***Infections:*** Sex during pregnancy requires partners to be cautious about how they engage. Some practices could put both the mother and the unborn at risk of infections. An example would be caused by combining anal sex with vaginal sex, which would bring bacteria to the pelvis and eventually affect the unborn.

4. ***Membrane Eruption:*** Deep penetration, as well as
    inappropriate sex positions, would lead to membrane
    eruption and possibly miscarriage. You should check
    out for signs of bleeding and pain during intercourse
    as warnings to these possibilities.

Best Positions for Sex During Pregnancy

Side by side: In this position, the partners face the same
direction lying by their sides with the man behind. It typically
resembles the typical posture made while they sleep, leaving
the bump comfortable and free. The penetration from behind
offers great clit stimulation and the ability to caress the
woman.

Woman on top: In this position, the woman takes full
control of the depth and pace of penetration. If she sits on
the flat-lying man, the bump remains suspended as she
allows the man to caress her and stimulate her clitoris.

Oral: It is a safer form of sex in pregnancy as it does not affect the formation in the pelvis. The fact that there is no penetration makes it comfortable for women who might be concerned with penetration at the time.

Anal: It does not involve vaginal penetration and still offers sexual stimulation through be nerve endings at the anus. You should not make contact with the vaginal openings when engaging in anal sex to avoid the spreading of bacterial infections.

Sex in Overweight

There are various ways that you could make your sex life enjoyable if you or your partner is overweight. Nothing should stop you from getting the best out of your partner through positivity and exploration. The first step about enjoying intimacy in your relationship should be disregarding the misconception associated with being overweight. Notably, issues arise in case one or all partners are overweight. You should find the best way to overcome those acts not only as a motivation but also a strong bond in the relationship. The following are considerations that you should make if you want to enjoy sex with an overweight partner:

1. **Be Positive:** With the acceptance that there is little you could do to change the situation, you are sure to find better ways to make your sex life more intimate. In addition, there should be no misconceptions to hinder you from making love to your partner as long as you are sure that they would enjoy it. Living positively and developing attitudes to support your life will make you most romantic to your partner.

2. **Own your Body Size:** You should not live in denial over the size of your body, thinking that it would prove unromantic to your partner. Note that being overweight does not make you ugly but makes you beautiful, depending on your partner's perception. For that reason, you should accept that you are overweight and be proud of it in order to make others find the beauty in you. Similarly, you should make your partner feel the same as they are overweight to alter their perception and eventually improve self-esteem.

3. ***Take Time***: The fact that your partner is overweight does not mean that they are different in their sex life. You should serve them in the same manner as you would treat a slim partner. In this case, you should take time when having sex with your partner, involving all the steps that are usually engaged in sex. Do not focus only on penetration, but you should take time for foreplay, and other forms of stimulation ton turn them on.

4. ***Handle with Pride***: It is common to find sagging and loose body part in overweight people, making you confused about how to react. It should not turn you off as it is the sole reason they f classified as overweight. You should treat the body parts as sensitive and needing a stimulating touch for sexual arousal. These parts include the buttocks, thighs, and the pubis. They are the most sensitive parts of obese people and may be the source of sexual stimulation and orgasm if caressed or rubbed.

5. ***No Desperation:*** As an overweight partner, you should not show desperation due to your body size, for it may hinder you from achieving sexual satisfaction. Instead, you should be content with yourself and make the best out of the activity. Expect to be treated as any other partner and believe that you deserve the best for you. Therefore, live within your means and find happiness and pleasure whenever your partner means to introduce them to you.

6. ***Position:*** There positions that might be difficult to try out for overweight couples. However, you could also explore additional positions that would help you attain orgasm and experience great intimacy. For example, the reverse cowgirl is perfect for it puts the bellies at different positions, making it easy6 for the woman on top to control the movement and penetration.

7. ***Additional Requirements:*** Overweight people require platforms that would support their total weight, especially when making angles and moves involved in intimacy. For that reason, you should outsource better equipment to enhance your sex life and feel relaxed whenever you jump into action. You require pillows to position your partner to make little efforts in the attempt of making sexual advances and stimulation. Similarly, you may need spring surfaced to balance your weights and reduce bodily friction.

8. ***Maintain Intimacy:*** There is no reason to leave your partner due to overweight or obesity. Various factors may have contributed to the condition, and it would be for your own good. Therefore, it is advisable to keep the love and intensify intimacy to make them feel appreciated and cherished. With the realization that sex is enjoyable in overweight, you would need to keep on having sex with your partner.

Pros of Sex in Overweight

Exercise: Sexual activity is part of an exercise, for it involves body movements and the application of pressure. Overweight partners can regulate their body mass index when they engage in sex, thus improving body performance.

Boosts Moods: Overweight people have difficulties managing their moods primarily due to the isolation and stigmatization they may face from society. Therefore they require attention and cuddling to rejuvenate the affection. Sex offers these advantages and helps them rethink their negativity.

Aids the Immune System: Sexual engagement among the overweight plays a significant role in enhancing their immune system. Orgasm helps release hormones used by the immune system to fight conditions in the body.

Regulates Blood Pressure: Sexual activities and orgasm involve a robust circulation of blood throughout the body.

As a result, the body maintains a healthy blood pressure preventing you from blood pressure-related conditions.

Boosts Self-Esteem**:** The act of caressing, cuddling, and penetrating an overweight partner may prove to be a great feeling for them, especially if they had faced isolation or stigmatization. They feel adored and find their value when they satisfy their partners sexually.

Long-Lasting**:** Being overweight is known to cause long term reaction among men. It might result in total satisfaction of the partner contrary to other men who last for seconds, leaving their partners hanging in sexual desperation.

Bonding**:** Intimate relationship among the overweight enhances the mutual bond and creates a loving environment for the partners. As a result, the partners remain connected, promising an enjoyable sex life ahead.

Cons

Positioning: Overweight partners may experience difficulties trying out various positions that may help them attain the utmost intimacy. The limited flexibility hinders the performance of positions such as 69. However, there are positions to try out as you advance to more complex ones.

Low Performance: Being overweight may hinder stamina development. It makes it impossible for partners to acquire physical strength that is vital in maintaining positions and keeping the orgasm longer. As a result, the partner may feel dissatisfied in sexual intercourse, leaving them in desperation.

Best Positions for Sex in Overweight

Reverse Cowgirl: In this position, the man lies flat on a bed as the woman turns while facing the same direction as the man. It helps the man make great stimulation on the G-spot while minimizing the contact between the bellies. Similarly, it allows the woman to take full control of the depth and pace of penetration.

Doggy: It is also a reverse version where the man penetrates from behind. The woman may bend and lean on a walk or any other platform for support. The position exposes the anus and the vagina to the man making it easy for him to access the clitoris and holding on her.

Missionary: The numerous variants of this position makes it easy to have sex with an overweight partner. The woman may lift her legs to place them on the shoulders of the man correctly, placing the clitoris for stimulation from the pelvis of the man. You could also p by placing the woman on the edge of a bed as the man stands supporting her legs and making thrusts.

Anal: It is a more straightforward position for the man who only needs to locate the anus. The nerve endings found in the anus play a significant role in stimulating the woman to relieving her duties in controlling their bodies.

Conclusion

The book discusses various ways in which couples could make different positions for ultimate stimulation and intimacy. The first step is also always the easiest; however, which is why the information you find in the following chapters is so essential to take to heart as they are concepts worth learning and practicing.

The initiation of an effective seduction as well as how well to do your foreplay. You will be guided on how to go about the endeavor and make substantial progress, especially if you have difficulties in your sexual life. You will find real-life instances that relate to your situations and experience. You need to acquire this information to enhance your performance in bed while nurturing your relationship. The numerous variants of sex, as well as the positions in which you could enjoy sex, leaves you with a variety of choices that would play a significant role in exploring ways to impress your partner.

Just because you've finished this book doesn't mean there is nothing left to learn on the topic, expanding your horizons is the only way to find the mastery you seek. It is your sole responsibility to internalize and practice your key take always for ultimate results. You may need to break down important points and prioritize them for easy and coordinated steps to action. Once you decide to try out some of the practices discussed to ensure you understand that your partner's consent is of utmost importance as it is a critical determinant in the acquisition of pleasure and stimulation.

Start with the easy sex positions as you work your way up through intermediate ones and, eventually, the advanced positions. A significant first step in making sexual stimulation should be through seduction, which expresses your swish to make sexual advances. Keep in mind that it can be hard to circumvent a partner who is unwilling to try out new sex positions or explore additional sex variants. Therefore, you should approach them with respect and love and persuade them of the need for trying out something different, and it may be a step to indulge in an ecstasy of sexual stimulation and orgasm.

BOOK 2

Sex Guide

*Make Your Partner Deeply Addicted To You With
Secret Tips to Transform Your Sex Life*

Marta Zielinska

Introduction

What is Intimacy?

There are different types of intimacy, and I will outline them for you before digging deeper into the intimacy that exists between couples. Intimacy, in a general sense, is defined as mutual openness and vulnerability between two people. There are different ways in which you can give and receive openness and vulnerability in a relationship. Intimacy does not have to include a sexual relationship (though it can); therefore, it is not solely reserved for romantic relationships. Intimacy can also be present in other types of close relationships like friendships or family relationships. Below, I will outline the different forms of intimacy.

Emotional Intimacy

Emotional intimacy is the ability to express oneself in a mature and open manner, leading to a deep emotional connection between people. Saying things like "I love you" or "you are very important to me" are examples of this. It is also the ability to respond in a mature and open way when someone expresses themselves to you by saying things like "I'm sorry" or "I love you too." This type of open and vulnerable dialogue leads to an emotional connection. In order for a deep emotional connection to form, there must be a mutual willingness to be vulnerable and open with one's deeper thoughts and feelings. This is where this type of emotional intimacy comes from.

Intellectual Intimacy

Intellectual intimacy is a kind of intimacy that involves discussing and sharing thoughts and opinions on intellectual matters, from which they gain fulfillment and feelings of closeness with the other person. For example, if you are discussing politics with someone who you deem to be an intellectual equal you may find that you feel a closeness with them as you share your thoughts and opinions and connect on an intellectual level. Many people find intellect and brains to be sexy in a partner!

Shared Interests and Activities as a Form of Intimacy

This form of intimacy is less well-known, but it is also considered a form of intimacy. When you share activities with another person that you both enjoy and are passionate about, this creates a sense of connection. For example, when you cook together or travel together. These shared experiences give you memories to share and this leads to bonding and intimacy (openness and vulnerability). This type of connection is usually present in friendships, in familial relationships and, more importantly, in romantic relationships. Being able to share interests and activities leads to a closeness that can be defined as intimacy.

Physical Intimacy

Physical intimacy is the type that most people think of when they hear the term "intimacy". It also involves other non-sexual types of physical contact such as hugging and kissing. Physical intimacy can be found in close friendships or familial relationships where hugging and kisses on the cheek are common, but it is most often found in romantic relationships.

Physical intimacy is the type of intimacy involved when people are trying to make each other orgasm. Physical intimacy is almost always required for orgasm. Physical intimacy doesn't necessarily mean that you are in love with the person you are having sex with; it just means that you are doing something intimate with another person in a physical way.

It is also possible to be intimate with yourself, and while this begins with the emotional intimacy of self-awareness, it also involves the physical intimacy of masturbation and physical self-exploration. I define sexual, the physical intimacy of the self as being in touch with the parts of yourself physically that you would not normally be in touch with. If you are a woman, these parts include your breasts, your clitoris, your vagina, and your anus. If you are a man, these parts include your testicles, your penis, and your anus. Being able to be physically intimate with yourself allows you to have more fulfilling sex, more fulfilling orgasms and a more fulfilling overall relationship with your body. Allowing someone to be physically intimate with you in a sexual way is also an emotionally intimate experience, regardless of your relationship with the person. Being in charge of your own body while it is in the hands of another person is very important and this is why masturbation is such a key element to physical intimacy.

You can think of physical intimacy as something that breaks the barrier of personal space. By this definition, this includes touching of any sort, but especially sexual intercourse, kissing touching and anything else of a sexual nature. When you are having sex with anyone, regardless of whether you have romantic feelings for them or not, you are having a physically intimate relationship with them. The difference between a relationship that involves physical intimacy alone and no other forms of intimacy and a romantic relationship is that a romantic relationship will also involve emotional intimacy, shared activities and intellectual intimacy is that a deep and lasting romantic relationship will need to include all of these forms of intimacy at once.

How to Increase Intimacy

For a romantic relationship to be successful, there must be several forms of intimacy shared between the partners. Without a combination of all of the forms of intimacy, there is nothing that sets a romantic relationship apart from an everyday friendship.

It is important to communicate about your needs for intimacy with your partner so that they know what is important to you and what you need from them for the relationship to be successful. Further, this must be tackled on a recurring basis since people will grow and change over the course of their relationship and both partners must be aware of the changes in the needs of their romantic partner. This is especially important in a long-term relationship, as being aware of when a person's intimacy needs change is important to maintaining a good level of intimacy and a deep connection.

Communication

Communication is the key in a relationship of any sort, but especially in a romantic relationship. Communicating is the only sure way to know where the other person stands in terms of their thoughts, feelings and needs. Being able to be vulnerable and open with your emotions is a requirement for any type of intimacy, and this involves being vulnerable and open about your needs for intimacy itself. It is necessary to share oneself with the other person in a relationship. This mutual sharing of yourselves is what will lead to intimacy in the first place as well as an increase in your level of intimacy.

Sometimes in a long-term relationship, you become so comfortable with each other that you begin to feel like you don't have to communicate with your partner as much as you once did. You may begin to feel like they can read your thoughts and your feelings, since you know each other so well. While this is a great point to reach in a relationship, this can sometimes lead to a breakdown in communication. It is important to maintain communication in order to avoid miscommunications or misunderstandings that can happen when both parties think that the other person can read their mind. The key here is to continue communicating, even if you think the other person knows what you are thinking or feeling without you having to say it. By doing this, you keep the lines of communication open in your relationship at all times. It is better to over-communicate than to under-communicate in a romantic relationship. This avoids any chance of miscommunication or misunderstanding that would be perpetuated by a lack of communication. By having misunderstandings go unresolved, this could lead to resentment and an overall breakdown in communication, which can reduce levels of intimacy in the relationship.

Orgasm

The orgasm is the culmination of a sexual relationship, a climax that produces a pleasant feeling of a sudden release of accumulated tension from the moment when the excitement phase begins. It is at that moment that a series of intense muscle spasms are generated that are highly pleasing, which helps the release of endorphins that occurs simultaneously.

Women experience orgasm in different ways, but usually, this is characterized by the fact that the acceleration of heart rate, breathing, and blood pressure reach their highest level and the vagina, uterus, anus, and muscles Pelvic bones contract between five and ten times at intervals of less than one second. However, some women may feel orgasm throughout their body and even multiple orgasms.

In the case of men, we must bear in mind that ejaculation and orgasm are not the same. You can ejaculate without experiencing orgasm. As in women, with orgasm, heart rate, breathing, and blood pressure are accelerated to the maximum, and muscle contractions occur in the pelvic area, as well as the prostate and seminal vesicles to produce the expulsion of the semen.

The orgasm lasts only a few moments and then enters what is known as the resolution phase in which there is a general relaxation of the whole body, normalization of blood circulation and breathing, and with it a feeling of great placidity, tiredness, and even drowsiness.

The lack of control over ejaculation, as in the case of premature ejaculation, can make a man unable to reach orgasm. Similarly, many women confess not to reach it regularly and even never (anorgasmia). It is very important that the couple talks about it because experimentation and information can improve their sexual practice and learn to control ejaculation in the case of men and enhance their excitement in the woman. Couples therapy can be a good option to solve this sexual dysfunction.

How Are Male And Female Orgasms Different?

The female orgasm

Contractions start at 0.8-second intervals and their number can vary greatly, decreasing after intensity, duration, and frequency. More than a localized response in the pelvis, it is a total response of the organism. Imagination is directly related to orgasm, the brain has a lot to do with it. With the penetration, the entire vulvar pyramid is mobilized synchronously and the G-spot and the clitoris are stimulated. Every woman has the physical ability to experience orgasms.

These are the symptoms of female orgasm :

- Greater increase in heart rate.

- Increase in breathing

- Increase in blood pressure.

- The subjective sensation of the explosion of pleasure.

- Contraction of the uterus.

Contraction of the orgasmic platform.

After the orgasm, there would be a recovery in the woman prior to the excitement. Although if it is restimulated before the sexual tension decreases, the woman is able to present several successive orgasms.

The Female Orgasm: Keys To Reach It

The female orgasm is not only achieved through penetration. It is highly recommended to explore the female body to discover erogenous zones that facilitate the task. In the case of sexual intercourse, preliminaries, oral sex, and other pleasurable practices can be the perfect vehicle to achieve an unforgettable orgasm. Meanwhile, it is also essential:

•   That your partner knows how to "work" better to "play" and experience things with you

to know oneself through self-exploration. So, if you want to enjoy your body and your areas of pleasure, try one of these useful toys.

1.   Physical manifestations of female orgasm

During orgasm:

•   the clitoris retracts,

- the vagina, the perineum and the uterus contract due to shaking

- the nipples harden

- the heart accelerates

the blood vessels dilate.

Everything is stimulated during this supreme pleasure with which women (and men, in their case) go mad. And it is normal because the orgasm involves secretion of endorphins, the molecule of happiness, which provides a feeling of unequaled well-being.

2.   How to achieve a female orgasm

In general, most women achieve orgasm when they stimulate sexual areas alone or in pairs:

- Preliminary caresses: activate your brain preparing for the moment of intercourse. These movements increase the pleasure much more and reach orgasm before.

- cunnilingus: is one of the techniques that most excites women and that will favor that if you have anorgasmia you can get to reach orgasm.

- masturbation: whether you do it yourself or your partner will get the genital area excited more easily.

penetration: through the penis the woman also reach orgasm. It is one of the most essential parts that lead us to intercourse, to the female orgasm, and also to the ejaculation of man.

But the best way to reach orgasm is knowing the body of one. We have different erogenous points that are able to make us feel in the seventh heaven, but you have to find them!

The solution: start in the discovery of the body:

- alone or as a couple,

- with sexual toys

without them, to detect the most moving areas.

3.   Different female orgasms

Vaginal orgasm: is achieved by stimulation of the Gräfenberg point or more commonly called "G-spot", located about 4 cm from the entrance of the vagina. It has a ball shape of less than one centimeter and increases in size with stimulation. It is located next to the bladder so it is not strange that after a vaginal female orgasm we feel like going to the bathroom. To sensitize, stimulate it regularly with gentle and repeated pressures with the point of the finger or with the help of a sex toy. Try these toys if you want to get an incredible vaginal orgasm:

•   Massager vibrator with 30 different modes.

•   Chinese vibrating silicone balls with remote control.

Vibrator with heat effect for women.

Clitoral orgasm : is achieved by stimulation of the clitoris. That is a small button located between the lips, anterior to the vagina. It is accessed very easily. It is very sensitive. You can reach orgasm with delicate caresses. Here we leave you a few positions that will facilitate the pleasant task. These are the best sex toys to stimulate the clitoris:

•   Satisfier Pro, clitoral sniffer.

•   Clitoral massager with cunnilingus effect.

Vibrator clitoris massager.

4.   The female orgasm, in figures

Clitorian orgasm: according to a study 95% of women come to him through masturbation and less than half, 45% share it with the male penis.

The vaginal orgasm: there are few women who manage to reach this orgasm. Only 30% have the pleasure of experiencing such pleasure. Although we all have a G-spot, we have to get "wake up" with multiple movements in this area. For this, there are positions that favor it: the missionary, with the legs of the woman on the back of the man or the greyhound, with which a deep penetration is facilitated.

5.   Female multiorgasm is possible

Although for some it is only a fantasy, the truth is that multiorgasm exists and is easier to achieve than it seems. The key is in:

*   know your own body,

*   know what is possible

*   put our mind on it,

*   lengthen the sexual climax (many times we do not achieve it because our partner lasts less than we would like),

*   go changing stimuli and erogenous zones

choose postures that really work with us

The Male Orgasm

There are between 3 and 10 contractions with an interval of 8 tenths of a second between each one, depending on how intense the response is. This means that an orgasm lasts on average between 4 and 8 seconds. Man experiences this physiological reaction as a wave of pleasurable sensations.

These are the symptoms of male orgasm :

- Greater increase in heart rate.

- Increase in breathing

- Increase in blood pressure.

- The subjective sensation of the explosion of pleasure.

- Contraction of the penis, urethra, and sphincter.

Expulsion of semen abroad.

After the orgasm, in man, there would be the recovery of the state prior to the excitement and the refractory period would begin, by which the man will not be aroused again after some time, something that can vary according to each person.

The Male Orgasm: Keys to Reach It

Orgasms during sex are better than during masturbation.

Ejaculating usually reduces the risk of cancer

Men who ejaculated more frequently (about 21 times a month) reduced their risk of prostate cancer by 20 %. This benefit is since during the orgasm, different hormones are released, such as oxytocin (known as lowering blood pressure, for example).

The male and female orgasms are more similar than it seems

Despite the difference in orgasm between men and women, there is no variation between the duration and intensity of orgasm concerning sex. What does offer opposition is that the orgasms are different in each person and can be divided into two main types: the usual orgasm, the most common, consisting of about 6-15 high-intensity contractions for about 20-30 seconds or orgasm prolonged, in which regular contractions are experienced after the initial orgasm, which can last between 30 and 90 seconds.

Male ejaculation is as fast as ...

The average speed of a man's ejaculation is 45 kilometers per hour. Taking into account that Usain Bolt runner holds the record of 44.72 kilometers per hour, the rate of ejaculation is faster than the fastest man on the face of the Earth.

Food for The Soul of Love

After that, many relations in my life became boring, I felt empty and frustrated, and I knew that I had recognized the smell of discontent. So I began to ask myself, "What's this deep feeling which I'm longing for?" "Why is love not sufficient?"

And so a new authentic understanding of the world came through my conscious mind: "Intimacy is the nourishment that feeds the soul of love."

Love has a soul that needs care and nurture. The nourishment of love is chosen from us every day, and freely given to someone else, in a way to open up a new world. When we agree with someone on the road of romance, we must flee away from habits and/or old familiar patterns that have obstructed our point of view.

You must reveal and do what you are most scared of, to attain a real intimacy. Your private, sacred life calls for exposure and vulnerability. Intimacy needs to take chances and go beyond your personal level of comfort.

You need to be able to run and lie down in the pit of yourself. It requires rigorous self-assessment to get to know you well, but once you have realized who you are, other people will be able to see the real yourself too.

Do you know why it has to be like this?

Because the foundation, from which love develops, is to be together with what YOU feel and desire.

There is no intimate relationship in which either party stays silent, loses, or betrays the other, and each party shares at the same level strength and insecurity, weakness and talent.

True intimacy happens when both people feel safe enough to be vulnerable. There is support for each other's weaknesses and celebration of each other's strengths.

Having said that, it is quite obvious how intimacy with your partner also affects the quality of your sexual relations. Intimate sex is a symmetrical experience, in which partners take turns pleasuring each other and looking at one another, at the same time.

It encourages partners to look at one another and communicate about what feels good through words, hand movements, gestures, and also noises.

The keys to intimate sex include feeling that you deserve sexual pleasure, achieving orgasm, and locking eyes with your partner.

Learning how to have a deep connection and more intimacy with your partner will protect the relationship from breakage, and will keep your bond strong.

Romance

Romance is the vital fuel that keeps a relationship lively, exciting and meaningful. Romantic gestures make feel, who receives them, desired, loved, cared for, and appreciated.

When we talk about romance, we don't have to think about movie scenes. Romance can be found in little gestures in our everyday life, it can identify in a gift, or a surprise, or in the right words spent in the right moment, but also with simple little attentions, for example, tucking the cover in bed or cooking dinner, etc.

Most people don't try to do anything romantic because they simply don't know how. However, there are no real secrets to romance, it's all about going with your heart. Most of the time, everything we need to know is right under our noses. And even just the desire to create romance is enough to get it started.

Romance is not standard; every single individual finds romance in different things. And here, the importance of intimacy is recalled again.

Thanks to intimacy, you get to know what your lover most desire, and, at the same time, your lover knows what YOU long for.

This means that romance is not a one-way system, and it is not, as we sometimes tend to think, something that should only be used by men to please or attract women. Romance leads the passion and brings the sexual intercourse to something much better than mere physical pleasure.

Romance has to be a constant in your universe, in both giving and receiving, and it's, together with intimacy, fundamental for the health of your sexual life.

Foreplay

Romance can definitely sweetly introduce you to a hot night in the bed. But you will get the best from your sexy night with the help of foreplay.

In terms of sex, foreplay is usually defined as any erotic stimulation preceding intercourse. However, it could be so good even before ending into a full intercourse. In fact, foreplay can be all you need to reach an orgasm.

But let's start slowly. The principal aim of foreplay is to slowly build an increased sexual desire, and it includes both physical and mental effects.

The physical responses to foreplay stimulation are the increase of blood pressure and heart rate, that lead to a dilatation in blood vessels and so the swell of both genitals. And in particular for the woman, the secretion of vaginal fluid that lubricates it and prepares it for penetration.

The psychological response is the establishment of intimacy, the tease of the imagination, and the reciprocal feeling of being desired. And your partner's positive response also makes you feel somehow successful and satisfied.

There is not a clear list of what sort of practice foreplay

includes, as it subjective and can literally be anything that turns you on. Foreplay can even start several hours' prior with a seducing text or footies under the table during a dinner or a quick pick at your underwear etc.

However, the most common types of foreplay are: kissing and caressing, vaginal stroking, handjob, and oral sex.

Kissing is a good start as it releases "feel good" hormones. There is no exclusion on which part of the body can be kissed, and it could be either gentle or more intensive, up to sucking and nibbling. The best thing to do is to start gently and slowly intensify it.

Caressing can be underestimated but, actually, the feeling could be very good for both who give and receives. Caressing the naked skin can be very satisfying to the touch and let your desire to reach the most intimate parts of the body. Be touched gives you shivers, makes your breath going faster, and increases your desire to be touched even more and also to touch in turn.

Caressing can then develop in breast stimulation, vaginal stroking, and handjob.

Vaginal stroking is fundamental for some women to be able to wet and reach the orgasm. It can begin over the clothes, caressing and rubbing the outer labia first, and gently moving into the inner labia with the fingertips. This part is very delicate but lubrication will make it easier. Fingers can be led to the vaginal opening to catch some fluid, or artificial lubricant can be used instead, and then carry on stimulating the clitoris. On the opening of the vagina, there are a lot of nerves, so tracing your fingers around and inserting some fingers in and out might feel very good. It's important to follow the guidance of the partner to be able to give the best pleasure experience, and it can actually be quite exciting to let her lead the movements with her hands on top of yours.

Hand job likewise, vaginal stroking can start with a bit of teasing over the clothes, outlining penis through the fabric, or cupping the hand over the clothed cock and letting it grind into it. To carry on would be ideal to remove the clothes, in a way to have a full range of movement. The penis stroke can be done in a different way, especially depending on its shape and conformation of the foreskin. The best option is to ask for feedback or to be guided with his own hand, regarding movements, tightness, speediness, etc. Even in this case, lubrication is fundamental, can be interesting to try to use artificial lubricants, or also spit or vaginal fluid. Testicles have a lot of nerve terminations, so it could be worthy to stimulate them with the other hand while stroking. Or also, both hands can be used to increase the strength and speed of the stroke. Once you can tell your partner is about to climax, focus the pressure more towards the head of their penis. Moreover, it is recommended to use long "milking strokes" once the climax is reached.

All the stimulations provided by hand stroking can be spiced up a lot more through oral sex. With oral sex, lubrication is not a problem anymore as saliva can make the most of it. However, you might be tented to use some flavored lubes to give a new taste to the experience.

There are a whole variety of ways to lick, suck and stimulate someone's sex with your mouth, so again the best option is to use your intimacy to get to know what your partner enjoys the most. You can still help yourself using the hand to, maybe to control how deep the penis goes in your mouth or to penetrate the vagina with the finger while licking the clitoris. In any case, for both males and females, the best way to give oral sex is to slowly increase the intensity of it.

Enjoying foreplay, you can build up a good level of intimacy and make the sexual relation much more pleasant. All you need to do is relax, create a sensual atmosphere, and communicate with your partner the more you can. And remember that everything has to be enjoyable and feel good for both of you.

Erotic Games

Respecting Your Partner

1.   Consent: The first way to ensure that erotic games and role play are a fun and safe experience for all that are involved is to ensure that everyone is on board with what is happening. This means that you ask for your partner before you start these games what is and isn't acceptable for them. Some partners will not like anal sex and it is important to respect those boundaries even in a game where one person is in the controlling or dominant role.

2.   Safety: Protecting yourself and your partner from sexually transmitted infections is an important step to take. If you have not been tested in a long time, it is important to make an appointment at a local clinic or your private doctor to make sure that you are free from any sexually transmitted diseases. If you are not, it is important to discuss those risks with your partner, as they should have consent in whether or not they have sexual interaction with someone who has a STI or STD. Should you not want to get tested, or have sex with multiple partners, it is important to wear protection.

3.   Birth Control: If you are not planning on having children with your partner, it is important to discuss the ramifications of the sex act and what you plan to do to protect against having children. There are many forms of birth control available from the temporary like condoms to more longer lasting options. Longer lasting options include birth control pills, rings and patches, and IUD's and implants. Each method has their own benefits and detriments so it is important to talk with your gynecologist about them. For men there aren't nearly as many options but you can talk with your physician to see what options are currently available including the more permanent options like vasectomies.

4.   Clarity: While this falls under consent it is important to ensure that you do not engage in sexual intercourse with someone that is clearly overly inebriated on alcohol or other substances. This is important because it shows respect for your partner by saying that you care about their mental well-being and understand that under the state of diminished mental capacity, they do not have the ability to make sound decisions about their sexuality.

5.   Relaxing: It is important to show respect to your partner by creating a relaxing atmosphere to have sexual activity that is relaxing for your partner, this does not exclude BDSM related dungeons and other facilities as those can be relaxing to depending upon your fetishes. A relaxing atmosphere is one that is free from judgement and ridicule of their body and fantasies as well as one that respects their safety and privacy concerns.

Erotic Games

Having taken the steps to ensure a respectful tone of events you are ready to begin your journey into increased eroticism. While these games aren't necessarily Tantra, they help to relax the mind and body and allow you to experience new sides of your partners sexuality. Here is a list of erotic games that you can try with your partner to decrease your inhibitions and allow yourselves to connect at a deeper level sexually. Try and choose three of these games that you want to try.

•	Make an appointment in a hotel bar or restaurant, as if you didn't know each other, then take a room in the hotel and love each other as if it were the first night.

•	Enjoy a candlelight dinner: the male partner brings a bouquet of fragrant flowers whose color reflects something he particularly appreciates in her, and she wears the dress that makes her feel most desirable.

•	Make love with your partner while someone else is watching.

•	Blindfold your partner and tie him and play with respect to his limits but in a BDSM context

•	Have sex outside, with respect to the laws of your location.

•	Try group sex

•	Go hiking and make love on the top of a mountain

•	Imitate animals having sex, choose exotic animals and have fun imagining ways that they might have sex.

- Try six different positions while trying to keep the insertion in place.

- Try anal sex.

- Caress your partner with scarves, feathers, and a silk cloth.

- Spread honey on the neck, on the breast, on the stomach, on the thighs and lick it off your partner.

- Try some consensual non-consent play where you pretend as if you are reluctant in the sexual act.

- Play doctor.

- Play naked twister

- Oil each other up and slide your oily naked bodies on top of each other while having sex

- Try your own fantasy

You may have thought of other ideas that are more exciting to you while listening to this list. It is also possible that none of these ideas seemed to your taste, try something different and see how well you can turn your partner on. Whatever you have decided after you have three ideas of what to try with your partner, get together and do the following:

1.   Tell each other which of the erotic games you would like to try.

2.   Invite your partner to try them with you.

3.   Allow your partner to propose variations to make them more comfortable.

4.   After you try each game exchange thoughts about the experience with each other.

This game should have helped you to discover your hidden fantasies. Your hidden fantasies are precious and allow us to make new discoveries about ourselves. These fantasies show us the way to new discoveries, they tell us where we can find the stimuli that make our reality more intense, where we can seek, discover and grow. In Tantra they say, "everything is allowed, there are no taboos, everything can be tried" meaning that everything that stimulates us and makes us feel good, will help to makes us feel more complete.

Beware, if you do these erotic games or other games of your choosing mechanically and without awareness or without grasping the energy that is released in the moment you will lose out on a valuable experience. This is a spiritual journey, like Tantra, remember to respect your partner and to discover new things about yourself. It is why the discussion about respect was so important because these games are to help us discover more about our partners, not just get off. These erotic games are to help you to challenge yourself and discover more about your partner, this is why Tantra is also called "the way of pleasure".

Along this route, it is good to always have some principles in mind:

1.   The fear is usually equal to the desire. If you have a fear of performing you have a desire to perform.

2.   The greater the fear, the stronger the desire.

3.   Following our desires, gives us an energy charge.

4.   For every wish fulfilled, we will discover others.

5.   The way of desires is not always linear. We may discover yearnings for the opposite of our desires as we fulfill a desire

The boundary between the known and the unknown, between habitual and new, is not a clear and distinct furrow, but a band of reality marked by two openings in front of us, that is, by two lines that invite us to go beyond them. Once we cross one threshold, we may find everything stimulating and while we may have fears, we will also have curiosity. We can always decide to go further or to withdraw from the game. If we go further and meet the second opening, fear may become overwhelming, but take time to decide to go further as you may regret it. But remember if you risk nothing, you gain no knowledge of yourself.

There is an art to exploring. The art consists in remaining between the two thresholds, in not falling back into the boredom of the known or into the abyss of dangerous lands, remaining in that intermediate belt where we feel intrigued and at the same time safe. This is how you discover new landscapes of yourself and dare to discover others.

Remember that we each have two souls in ourselves; one that pushes and the other brakes. If after some erotic game we note that the band between the two thresholds seem very narrow, it means that in us the shy part and the courageous part are in conflict.

Exorcising Inhibitions Exercise

To start a negotiation between these two parts of yourself there is an exercise you can try. The exorcising inhibitions exercise allows you to imagine your shy side and your brave side as two distinct characters. Here is how to do this exercise.

1.   Imagine two characters each a few feet apart and a few feet in front of you. Imagine them well, give them details and characteristics. Maybe the brave side is played by a fierce knight with a big sword and the shy side is played by a humble stable boy. Whatever you imagine, imagine it in detail. Give them voices and gestures, in your mind.

2.   Observe the characteristics of both of these characters.

3.   Ask yourself in which instances are these characters correct about their assumptions of things.

4.   If at the beginning you are more attracted to on character over the other ask yourself why and think of the possible negative consequences of always listening to the one character. Maybe we would become bank robbers if we always acted out of daring, or maybe we would have never taken a chance to ask out our partner if we never took a chance like the shy character would have liked. Imagine what it would be like if they were each alone, without the other to temper them.

5.   Ask yourself what they gain if they are together and how they support each other.

6.   Imagine yourself as the shy side moving slowly to the place where the brave hero stood. Imagine him shedding the skin of the shy stable boy to become the courageous knight bringing with him all the good qualities that come with being timid and taking on all the good qualities of being brave.

7.   Begin to feel like the new character, the new character is a person that is no longer in conflict with the two parts of their personality but knows how to navigate the world with both their timid and brave sides in harmony.

By trying this exercise, you will find that you are able to understand why you must remain between the two thresholds of your personality. That by following the direction of the two parts of you that you find balance. The more you manage to integrate the two parts of yourself the less inner conflict you will have. You will begin to move in the high energy area that is the world between the two thresholds. This does not just apply to erotic games but to all the challenges and changes that we encounter on life's journey.

Essential information from the Kamasutra

One of the best-known works of the east is the Kamasutra of Vatsyayana. Other well-known books are that of the Kokasastra of Kokkoka, the Tibetan Kamasastra and the Chinese Fangchungshu. These are all books that intend to enlarge the map of eroticism, find new ways of uniting, and help people get out of their habits. There is; however, danger in taking them as simple techniques as if they are sex gymnastics. These are positions that are intended to induce certain moods and atmosphere to create a sense of togetherness.

Some care must be taken with experimenting with new positions. The six most important factors to consider to ensure quality energy charge and a high degree of awareness when making love are the following:

1. Breath: We must first evaluate if you can breathe freely in a particular position, if this is not taken care of not only will we not be able to charge our energy we can run the risk of suffocation.

2. Pelvic Movement: Ensure that you can manage to rotate it and move it freely

3.   Hands: Make sure that your hands are free to touch and caress your partner even when you are not having penetrative sex.

4.   Position: Ensure that it is a relaxing position to keep for a prolonged period, again evaluate if you can support either your own or your partner's weight in this position.

5.   Look: Can you look into your partner's eyes and communicate to them freely with all your heart through nonverbal communication.

6.   Support: Is this a good position to have support in, can you find a more supportive position to hold.

As for positions in these books, they can easily be divided into four broadly defined categories.

1.   man above, woman below

2.   woman above, man below

3.   from behind

4.   tantric positions

Each of these positions gives a particular color to the sexual act. In the first two positions, the "above" and the "below" are often connected with controlling and submitting, given that the partner above is favored in driving the rhythm and the movement. In regards to these above and below positions it is worth trying the various types of positions that are available. Try them and see how both you and your partner feel.

Positions from behind, or "behind", usually solicit a very corporeal, animalistic, passionate sexuality. These are positions that allow you to make more love at the 1st level of the chakra, also known as pure sex with a deeper sense of penetration depending on the length of the vaginal canal and the penis. Furthermore, depending upon the angle, these positions can stimulate the g-spot more easily.

The Tantric positions usually have the partners on the same level and are very useful for tantric sexual exercises.

One such position that has an advantage in Tantric sexual relations is Scissors position. This position is suitable for making love in a relaxed way for a long time.

In this position the man is able to adjust the balance between excitement and the containment of his energy charge while slowly moving the pelvic region. He will be able to control any rapidly approaching orgasm by adjusting the rhythm and slowing it down to give him a moment to charge and release some of that sexual energy that has built inside of him. Another advantage of this position is that it allows the woman to reach her clitoris with her hand and allows her to excite herself easily. Finally, this position allows both partners to remain in good visual contact and have their hands free to caress each other during their union.

How the Scissors Position is Performed:

The male and female lie joined at the genitals both of them with their legs intertwined but their bodies aligned in opposite directions, they are head to toe and toe to head.

However, it is important to remember that in any position it is important to communicate with your partner based on the six factors above as any position can become uncomfortable depending upon your body, feelings or any thoughts that may arise during your union.

Lubricants, Gels, Toys, and their Role

Lubes can sometimes be essential. The vagina can sometimes fail to self- lubricate enough for both of you to enjoy the intercourse session. Lubricants and gels are especially necessary whenever you are getting into anal penetration, simply because the ass is not capable of self-lubricating like the vagina.

In a nutshell, lubricants make sex more enjoyable and comfortable for any gender. The juices excreted by the vagina and saliva, most of the time, will not give sufficient lubrication to get the job done correctly. Even if you have some alone time and feel the mood to masturbate, whether it is with your hand or using tools, lubricants will help take your experience to a whole other level.

You need to have in mind that you cannot just use any lubricant or gel you find; you need to get one that is explicitly made for sexual intercourse. You can look for a wide array of lubes in a majority of drug stores and in any sex shop you can find. Technology has made buying lubes even easier and more convenient because you can order online from the comfort of your home and have it delivered to you; in some cases, delivery can be also made within the hour!

There are three main types of lubricants or gels that are available in the market, all of them come in various brands and scents, and we will have a look at them separately in this chapter.

Water-Based Lubricants and Gels

One of the best features of water-based lubricants that makes them the preferred choice of many is that they do not easily stain fabrics, and cleaning them up is quite easy. They are available in a wide array of tastes, textures, ingredients, and consistencies. These lubricants are also very much compatible with all the materials used to make sex toys, as well as those that are used to manufacture both latex and non-latex condoms.

You need to note, however, that the majority percentage of these water-based lubricants are manufactured using glycerin, and this can make some people uncomfortable or even cause problems. A large number of women attribute to glycerin, the cause of an imbalance in the yeast levels in their vagina and also yeast infections. Despite this risk does not affect anal sex; when it comes to anal sex, there are some people who find that lubricants that contain high levels of glycerin tend to stimulate their bowel movements, and so they prefer to avoid them.

No need to worry, though, as there is an increasing number of different lubricants that do not contain any glycerin, and also, there are some that do not even contain parabens.

In terms of texture, water-based lubricants completely cover a good variety. They are available in varying levels of liquidity, ranging from super-thick, thick, medium, and also thin. Any lubricant can greatly facilitate penetration, but thick and super-thick lubricants are more efficient and so better suited for anal penetration. The reason is that they possess a consistency that is very similar to hair gel. They tend lasting longer and also protect the gentle rectal tissue by acting as a cushioning layer.

Depending on your preferences, if you may like to put either your hands, sex toys, or even a penis in your mouth after they have come in contact with a lubricant or gel, you might want to purchase a lubricant that has a pleasant taste, or at least, a flavor that you can stand. Some plain water-based lubricants taste of chemicals or have a sour taste that is a dreadful turn-off.

For this reason, a quite number of sexual lubricants that are flavored have been introduced on the market, and if you are not lucky enough to find your taste of choice in the first attempt, you may have to taste quite a number of flavors before to find your favorite.

Among all the different quality, the current trend feature, regarding water- based lubricants, is the warming ability. These lubricants create a warming effect upon contact. This effect is generated by a variety of different ingredients, for example: Acacia honey or any of its derivatives

Menthol

Cinnamon bark extract. (It is the most natural among them all)

The honey and menthol generate a warming feeling that makes blood rush to the genitals, thereby assisting in the arousal process.

As far as lubricants are concerned, whether or not you like it depends on your personal preferences and what you find comfortable. Some people believe that they love the way it causes their private parts to tingle; others have horror stories about it (probably they did not know about the possible side effects of glycerin). A vast majority of women prefer warming lubricants because they have an element of protection for the vagina, but at the same time, many people find that they get an overwhelming feeling whenever they use this warming lubricants for anal penetration.

Silicon-Based Lubricants

Also, lubricants and gels that are made using silicon are quickly becoming popular among consumers. Some brands that have silicone-based lubricants and gels are System JO Original, ID Velvet, Swiss Navy Silicon, Eros gel, Wet platinum, and KY Intrigue. Just like water-based gels and lubricants, silicon-based lubes also do not stain fabrics. They are odorless and are more expensive than water-based lubricants and gels because they are usually more concentrated and, therefore, can go a long way, they do not dry up as fast as water-based ones, and so you can use less lube a time. A lot of people typically have a liking to silicon's slick texture and its fantastic quality of not being tacky or even sticky like their water-based counterparts. Some people claim that this sleek texture of silicon gives a lot of less friction, making it a better option for anal sex.

Silicon-based lubricants work well with both latex condoms and non-latex condoms and with a select number of materials used to make sex toys, including glass, rubber, metal, and hard plastic. Conversely, sex toys that are made using silicon are entirely incompatible with silicon-based gels and lubricants as they get damaged. The only way that silicon sex toy lovers can get to lubricate them with silicon-based lubricants and gels is by wrapping them up with a condom. If you like to get a little wild in the shower or a swimming pool, silicon-based lubes and gels are the best option because, unlike water-based lubricants, they remain slick underwater too. This quality makes them the best choice for getting the job done in such wet scenarios.

Oil-Based Lubricants and Gels

Oil-based lubricants are the least preferred and chosen by the consumers and also the least reliable. The simple reason behind this is that they are very messy and leave behind nasty stains on whatever they come in contact with. They are also responsible for the breakage of latex condoms and the sex dolls.

Moreover, the most significant risk that these lubes and gels have is that they have a tendency to cling to the walls of the vagina, and they cannot get easily flushed out of the body. This is very unhealthy to the woman because it becomes a perfect spot where bacteria can breed, and this will eventually result in a vaginal infection.

Even if you use these lubes for anal sex, they can always make their way to the vagina, and the result is going to be the same. The best thing you can do to spice up your sex life is to use oil and vegetable-based lubricants for their intended purpose like massages, and not for sex.

Men can eventually use them for masturbation, but they need to make sure to rinse off their penis thoroughly before they can penetrate someone else.

How to Properly Use Lubricants and Gels

Using lubricants and gels is a pretty straight forward process. You need to apply it on whatever you need to insert, be it a penis, finger, or a sex toy, then slide it in. You need to remember that water-based lubricants and gels dry up quicker, and therefore you should use a lot of it and also be prepared to refill it halfway through. Silicon-based lubes do not dry up quickly, and therefore you can comfortably use it sparingly. You can have it around, though, to keep it spicy. A box of baby wipes or pocket tissues can also come in handy to wipe out any extra gel, spillages, or any other accidents that may occur.

When it comes to anal sex, sometimes it can become challenging to get the lube to where it is supposed to get. Luckily, two commodities are available in the market that can help to solve this problem.

1. There is a soft plastic tube of the Astroglide Gel that has a long neck, and it is called the Astroglide Gel Shooter. What you need to do is to gently rip off the top and slip the neck inside the butt hole and squeeze the lube inside the anus.

2. Secondly, there is the Lube Shooter, and this is typically a non-reusable plastic syringe, and for safety, it has a flared base. There are two ways of refilling it:

Take off the cap that is on the tip and place the tip in a bottle of lube. Pull up the plunger and draw the lube into it like a syringe.

Pour your favorite lube into the barrel after removing the plunger. You need to know, however, that this method can be a little messy. Once it is full, lube the syringe tip and gently insert it into the ass. Push down the plunger so that the lube can be released into the ass. At your pleasure, you can refill the shooter and repeat the process. Make sure then to dispose of it after the use.

Sex Toys

If you are never so keen on the use of sex toys, you should know that there are many good reasons to start doing it.

Using sex toys to enhance sexual pleasure and orgasm can help you to sleep, boost immunity, relieve pain, reduce stress, and boost your brain power.

Also sex toys, like vibrators, are a great way to introduce the concept for a girl who has never masturbated before. Or a woman who has never been able to have an orgasm.

Or for a young man to his first experiences, a sexy doll can be a great way to learn about his body and sexuality, improve all the involved muscles, and learn new things.

Obviously, sex toys are suitable for both solo explorers and curious couples. However, if you are not sure of what can be actually pleasurable for yourself, you may want to explore the option on your own before sharing the experience with your partner. Get acquainted with how they work and feel. In this way, you will avoid awkward or embarrassing situations.

Furthermore, sex toys can be the catalyst to reinvigorate sexual relationships for long-term partners. In fact, for both men and women, one benefit of introducing sex toys into the dynamic is to open up a dialogue about sex and about what they enjoy as individuals and a couple.

It may be something that they haven't tried before due to embarrassment or fear of purchasing items, and they may find that their sex lives could benefit from this new openness. So once you are comfortable to share the experience with your other half, you can start this new adventure. Make sure to approach a conversation about sex toys with 'I'd like to try this with you,' to ensure that it's an inclusive experience, as some partners might be concerned that they might be replaced or feel inadequate, so tread gently.

As a matter of fact, sometimes, if you bring something new and exciting into your sex life, it makes you bond with your mate even more. Clearly, shopping for a new play item for many pairs can be a big turn-on. You can say sexy things to each other while searching between the shop racks, disclose what you want about a certain product and taunt each other.

A guy I met, every Christmas orders his wife a special new gadget with a personalized card; it's now their tradition. For more than fifteen years, they had an enjoyable and fulfilling sex life.

One thing is sure: there is plenty of more fun to come once you have made your purchase. Things like swings, blindfold, relaxation oil candles and G- spot devices could expand your sexual arsenal to new activities. And toys also can set the stage for imaginary role games.

Moreover, Sex toys can bring you an "extra set of hands" in your bedroom, enabling you to do two or three things at once! Imagine that you can accomplish to her vaginal penetration, clitoral stimulation, and anal gratification at the same time.

If the position you are on doesn't allow you to have access to other parts of the body that you might like to stimulate too, a vibrator may be there to help you. For example, if you want to play concurrently with his cock, ass, and nipples, a vibrator or nipple clamps will help you to cover all of your favorite hot spots.

As well as offering pleasure and fun, sex toys can be a useful adjunct to medical treatment. Some medications can impact sexual function and pleasure in both men and women, including cancer treatments, antidepressants, antihistamines, blood pressure, and heart medicines. This can be countered with the aid of sex toys.

For example, women can find sex toys to be helpful in the treatment of menopausal symptoms such as vaginal atrophy, vulvar/vaginal pain and tightness, lack of arousal and low libido.

Vibrators can create different types of sexual stimulation, which can be beneficial when there is a decreased sexual sensation, low libido or an inability to enjoy orgasm.

Using a slim vibrator can help to stretch the tissues of the vagina to enable penetration without pain, and the vibrations increase the blood flow to the walls of the vagina, promoting healing, stimulating nerves, and improving the lubrication.

There are a number of sexual problems in men as well, that may be helped by using specific sex toys. These include erectile dysfunction, premature ejaculation, lack of libido and post-surgical problems for a variety of conditions.

Constriction rings can help a man maintain his erection for longer, making it firmer and also delay ejaculation. Specially-designed male vibrators can help men to gain an erection and stimulate nerve endings. They can also help with delayed ejaculation as they offer a different sexual sensation to manual masturbation.

Furthermore, there are some sex toys designed for pelvic muscle training. The activity of pub coccygeal muscles (also known as the PC muscles) has a main part in male and female sexual wellbeing. From the pubic bone, the PC muscles go to the tailbone to protect the cervix and intestine. Such muscles contract spontaneously for both men and women when you get sexually excited or rhythmically during orgasm. Improving their pc muscles with workouts, men may enhance their prosthetic fitness, learn to control and postpone ejaculation, reduce incontinence, sustain stronger erections and have more flexibility during intercourse.

PC muscles for women can be strained, damaged, and atrophied by diabetes, pregnancy, and birth, during sexual abstinence, or as part of aging. With the right exercise of the pelvic muscles, women can obtain many positive results:

- A stronger sexual tolerance

- Improved satisfaction through clitoral stimulation, or vaginal and anal penetrations.

- A better-controlled orgasms.

- Maintaining the urinary tract healthier.

- The control and the progressive decreases of incontinence.

- Easier pregnancy and birth.

After we have evaluated all the positives of introducing a sex toy into your life, we will now discuss specifically about some sex toys for pleasure use.

Just remember, when choosing a sex toy, to select 'skin-safe' products made from silicone, toughened glass, metal or ABS plastic, as some are made from materials that may be detrimental to sexual health. Jelly and rubber, for example, are both porous, therefore difficult to clean, and they degrade over time, so avoid those and latex.

And also, make sure to select the right lubricant, following the guide I gave you in the previous paragraphs.

Wand Vibrators

Vibrators are probably the most common type of sex toy; wand vibrators offer vibrations at a higher RPM. They work really well for people who enjoy a strong sensation, or who have difficulty getting fully aroused without intense stimulation. Wand vibes can also be used for applying stimulation to your non-nether regions—they double as a back and shoulder massagers, a teasing tool to trace on someone's body, or a very intense nipple toy.

One of the bestsellers is the Europe Magic Wand.

Clitoral Vibrators

Considering most women and people with vaginas (around 70%!)

can't <u>orgasm</u> through internal stimulation alone, Clitoris vibrators are among the most popular sex toys. They're typically very small, less phallic-shaped, and are intended specifically for the clitoris.

There is a big range of shapes and sizes; some of them are "hand free" like the <u>Eva II</u> by Dame that has wings that wrap around the labia so that the vibration is applied directly to the right point. Others have a shape of a bullet, and they're great for really precise stimulation and focusing vibrations exactly where you want them most. And finally, there are also clit <u>vibrators that look like everyday objects like lipstick and/or a necklace</u>, so that you can keep them always with you without anyone noticing it.

Clitoral suction toys

Clit suction toys use air pressure to create a gentle sucking. They create gentle throbbing and sucking sensations around the clitoris, which help to increase circulation, boost arousal, and give an 'out of this world' orgasms. They're a very, very different sensation than vibrators; people who really love oral sex or who find vibration patterns too intense tend to like these more.

One of the most sold it's called Satisfyer Pro 2. Satisfyer is a big name in this corner of the sex toy industry. Their Pro 2 model boasts 11 different intensity levels, an ultra-quiet "whisper" mode, and is 100-percent waterproof, meaning nothing should get in the way of you and your Orgasm.

Dildos and Strap On

A sex toy is qualified as a dildo if it is anything vaguely phallic shaped that is meant to simulate penile penetration. Dildos can be made from a number of different materials and are shaped like an erect human penis. They can be any length or girt; there are ones that are two inches and ones that are monster- sized.

There are also wearable dildos called strap on. Strap-on dildos are a fantastic sex toy for couples and can be used for pegging, lesbian sex, double penetration, or to help with erectile difficulties. The first part of a strap-on setup is the harness. Many types of harnesses are available, with different features and drawbacks. Some of those dildos, however, do not need a harness (like a double dildo).

G-spot and A-spot toys

G-spot toys make it easy to apply firm pressure to the <u>G-Spot</u>, thanks to their slight curve or expertly positioned bump. The A-spot is an erogenous zone a little further back than the G-spot and technically known as the anterior fornix erogenous zone. There are toys specifically meant for A-spot stimulation. Typically, they look like long, narrow variations of the G-spot toys. Both kinds of toys can be vibrating or not.

Rabbit Vibrators

A rabbit toy is a combo of an external vibrator and a G-spot toy.

It has an external part that usually looks like rabbit ears that provides vibration to the clitoris, while a second attachment goes inside the vagina for G-spot stimulation. This toy is best for people who find duel sensations pleasurable, or those who want to experiment with <u>blended orgasms</u>. Make sure the toy you purchase allows you to control the vibration patterns of both parts separately because usually, the G-spot and clitoris need different intensities. The Jack Rabbit by Calexotics is one of the best options to consider.

Butt Plugs

Butt plugs are great for experimenting with anal play. They can teach your body to accept anal penetration and train your sphincter to relax around different sized toys. They have a flared base, which means they can be used safely without being attached to something like a harness.

They typically go in and stay there to give a sustained feeling of fullness, and they're awesome for stimulating the ring of nerves around the anus.

Anal Beads

Unlike butt plugs, which, as we said, typically go in and stay in, anal beads provide the sensation of the anal sphincter opening and closing. As you insert the beads, the sphincter opens up and then closes, giving you a teasing sensation if you like to use them while stimulating your penis or vagina, either with intercourse or anything else, pulling them out as you climax can create a more intense orgasm.

Cock Rings

Cock rings were originally created to give people with penises a longer, fuller erection because they compress the blood vessels, and they can also make the penis more sensitive. Now, there are also vibrating cock rings which offer the same effect, while providing a boozy sensation to the wearer and the partner being penetrated. They're also a great way to turn dildos into vibrating dildos for strap-on sex. One of the best products on the market is the Lelo Tor 2, as recommended by GQ magazine.

Masturbation Sleeves

A masturbation sleeve is a flexible tube used to enclose the penis and enhance masturbation. Masturbation sleeves have one or two openings (on one end or either end) and may include different internal texture to increase sensation. Masturbation sleeves are offered in a variety of materials, such as plastic, silicone, and thermoplastic elastomers (TPE), a rubber-like material. Some masturbation sleeves are designed to look and feel like a vagina, which is why they are often called pocket pussies. Male masturbation sleeves are used to increase the pleasure of solo play. That said, they can also be used with a partner.

On the market, there are some disposable sleeves called Tenga Eggs, which are very popular and inexpensive. Also, there are some innovative kinds of sleeves that have been improved to be hand free or to simulate oral sex. One of these is the Tenga's Onacup; the company describes this toy as "a vacuum- fired deep throat blow-job you can keep on your bedside table."

Prostate Toys

Built for people with prostates (of the male sex, for the most part), the function of these toys is to provide direct sensation to the prostate—some vibrate, some do not. They're a slender, curved toy very similar to G-spot toys. They provide direct sensation to the prostate, and are a great option for people who want to explore prostate play but doesn't want to use their hands." Lelo is one of the best-known brands for this kind of toy.

Sex Dolls

A sex doll is a type of sex toy in the size and shape of a sexual partner. The sex doll may consist of an entire body with face, or just a head, pelvis, or other partial body, with the accessories (vagina, anus, mouth, penis)
for sexual stimulation. The parts are sometimes vibrating and may be removable or interchangeable.

This is obviously an enjoyable solo sex toy; however, Couples buy dolls as well as singletons. Couples sometimes find the dolls a safe way to introduce another partner in their sexual relationship, as in this way, there are no emotions, like it would be with a third real partner. Using a sex doll for a threesome, it's sexual exploration without cheating.

Also, Dolls are sometimes introduced as sexual surrogates when one partner is unable to enjoy sex, often for health reasons, but the couple does not want any outside lovers.

How To Talk Dirty In An Erotic Way

When it comes to talking erotically with your partner, there is a certain level of intimacy that must be achieved. This intimacy is very important, because otherwise, your words will fall flat, and will be deemed almost ridiculous in a way. You have to set the mood, and make sure that you maintain it as well. There are several ways you can do this, but you cannot set the mood without first gaining confidence.

Why is Confidence Important?

If you do not have confidence, it can bring an air of uncertainty to your bedroom endeavors. This is something that you would find yourself struggling to overcome. First impressions are everything, and if you are not confident the first time you try to introduce erotic conversation, you could turn your partner off from it for a long time.

Confidence is the foundation for anything in life. If you want to achieve any of your goals, confidence will get your farther than even knowledge, because you will not constantly second guess yourself. Doing this can lead to many different mistakes that will cause you possibly to not achieve your goal. It is essential that you have confidence when you are trying to dirty talk. It will make your words appear to come out effortlessly, and to help you encourage your partner to join in. When you seem confident, your partner will use your confidence to help build theirs.

Confidence is sexy. It is the drive behind what gets the libido up and running. You have to be able to have confidence for dirty talk, because it is all about being sexy, and you cannot pull off sexy without confidence. No confidence means an ineffective attempt at wooing your partner with words.

Life becomes easier to handle. The less you try to tear yourself down, the more you love yourself. This makes it easier to face every day, because you are not your own worst enemy. When you genuinely believe in yourself, you can find a lot more to enjoy in life. This makes life a lot easier to look forward to.

You won't rely on outside validation. The most attractive quality in a person is their ability to be sure of themselves. These people do not need validation from others, and find themselves quite appealing in their own rights. They feel this way without being overtly cocky, and they have a great balance of self-assurance.

You will not be afraid of the good things in life. By not being afraid of these things, you will be less likely to sabotage your attempts to find happiness, because you will know that you deserve them. This helps in relationships, because you will not try to push the other person away, and will want to bring them closer. You will be confident when you find the right person, and will want to show them the real you, rather than trying to get them to tell you who to be.

Why Might Confidence Be Lacking?

Some people just seem to ooze confidence in everything that they do. They feel as if they are meant to do whatever it is they set their mind to. When they go for something, it just seems to fall in their lap. You may not have this much confidence, and that is okay. The important question is why you feel that way.

Insecurities run rampant in the world. Some people are told from a young age that they are not good enough, and it is engrained in their mind. For some people, the entire world could tell them that they are good enough, but it just takes one trusted person to tell them that they aren't to wreck their self-confidence. Whatever the reason, not having confidence can mean disaster for you.

Some people seem to feel like they must be perfect at everything, including looks to have confidence. This is not the truth. No one is perfect at everything, and trying to be can leave you a nervous wreck. This is not a good way to introduce dirty talk. You must go in having confidence in order to cover up any words that may not have been phrased properly. You must have confidence so that you are not dissuaded when it doesn't go perfectly, because there will be those days.

Confidence is something that not everyone has naturally, and that is okay. There is a way to build your confidence, even if you do not seem to have any. You just have to make sure that you follow through with all of these steps. When you are trying to build your confidence, it is key to remember that it does not always happen in one day, and you have to work hard at it, and on yourself as well. You cannot give up just because you do not find yourself the best in the world after trying for a day or two to build your confidence. It does not work like that, and that can cause a lot of people to give up, because they want the easy way out.

Giving up would be social torture to yourself. You have to keep working on it in order to make yourself a better person, and a better partner. No one wants to constantly have to reassure their partner that they find them attractive and sexy. You have to be able to assure yourself, because you want people to want you, not feel like they have to want you.

If you give up, you could find yourself in a bit of a tough spot, and not able to achieve what you wanted to achieve in your goals of becoming a more open person in the bedroom. You must have confidence.

The Steps to Gaining Confidence

Confidence generally takes some work, so do not worry if you are not the most confident person in the world. You can learn how to gain confidence in yourself with these steps. These steps are designed to help even the most self-conscious gain enough confidence to be more adventurous in the bedroom.

The first step to gaining confidence is to simply fake it. That's right, pretending that you have confidence will eventually trick your brain into thinking that you really are confident. This will make it easier to build up your real confidence. When you fake confidence, it will have other people noticing that you seem surer of yourself. This validation will show you that it really works. When you look good, you feel better, and that is the mentality that faking it uses. It may seem silly, but "fake it till you make it" is not a saying for no reason. It applies here too. Faking it does not necessarily mean acting like the jock in a cheesy nineties movie, it simply means believing in yourself a little more, or at least acting like you do.

Setting the mood

It is important to set the mood with your partner. You have to make sure that you are making them comfortable, and turning them on at the same time. There are several things that you can do to set the mood. The first is communication.

Communication

Communication will open the door to being able to dirty talk your partner. If you can communicate about anything with your partner, you will be able to set the mood a lot easier, because you can both talk about whether it is the right time to engage in sexual conversation. If you are not able to communicate, sometimes one of you may not be in the mood, and setting the mood will be futile, because it will feel forced.

It is true. Communication is the key to any successful relationship. Especially when it comes to something like Kamasutra. It is the duty of each partner to ensure that they are satisfying their lover, but it is also their duty to let their lover know how they are feeling.

Humans are not mind readers, and often do not know what you are thinking. You have to be open with your partner, and allow your partner to be open with you, otherwise you will have some serious issues. A lot of times people are not open because their partners shut them down, and get angry at criticism, so they feel that they are not able to be open. You have to encourage communication both in and out of the bedroom.

In the bedroom, make your partner feel comfortable with vocalization. If they are nervous let them know that it is not silly, and you like knowing that what you are doing feels good, or if it doesn't feel good, you want to know so that you can make the proper adjustments. You should also lead by example. A lot of times one partner is very vocal, while the other is silent, you should both be vocal. Do not be afraid of shouting or screaming in pleasure. Also, do not be afraid to tell your partner what doesn't feel good. You can make it less harsh by asking them to change something nicely, rather than saying that hurts. This way there is no killing of the mood.

You also need communication in your everyday life as well. When your partner upsets you, you should tell them rather than bottling it up until it becomes a fight. You should also tell them if they are doing something you like. Too many times in the real world, everyone talks about what they don't like, but no one talks about what they do like. Yet in the bedroom it is the opposite. You should definitely find a balance in both.

Communication is a necessary part of your everyday life. Even if it is just talking about your day. Many relationships fail because there is not enough communication to keep the passion alive. You want to tell your partner everything. When they ask how your day was, it is because they want to know. The do not want a one word answer such as "good." When they ask you, be free with the information. Tell them every little boring detail, and then ask them about their day. Revel in what they are saying to you, even if the words are unimportant. Your lover will be happy knowing that even if they had a really boring day, you want to know about it. Things like that are the little things that make the world go round, and truly make a relationship work. Communication is a show of love, and it will help keep your love strong. Use it to its fullest power.

Making Your Partner Comfortable

The biggest way to get your partner comfortable is communication. However, there is one other thing you can do to help get in the mood. Make them feel good about themselves. Help boost your partner's self-confidence. This will help relax them and allow them to relax knowing you find them as attractive as they feel they need to be to reciprocate. To do this, you simply have to compliment them.

Compliment Them

A lot of the time, being self-conscious is a big problem. People are so caught up in self-image that it is hard to be confident in your own skin. A lot of that has to do with the way bodies are portrayed in the media. The world has this idea of perfection, and expects everyone to reach it. Even if your partner does not say it out loud, chances are, they have a poor self-image. Everyone struggles with some form of insecurity, and there are not enough compliments going around in the world these days.

Find five things about your partner that you like visually, and five things about them that you like outside of their physical appearance. Throughout the day, compliment them on these things. Make sure they understand that your compliments are sincere. It is best to look them in the eyes when you compliment them. Compliments will make them feel like they are on top of the world.

Do not overdo the compliments though, because they can begin to feel insincere. Make them heartfelt and true. Do not use them just for getting ready for sex. You should be complimenting your partner on a regular basis. Build up their self-esteem so that they feel like they are powerful. You may be surprised at the wild side they could unleash when they feel like they are truly good for you. It is quite the sight to behold.

Setting the mood will help set the stage for intimate conversation. You want to have the right mood when you are trying to get your partner to feel comfortable. There is no specific time when setting the mood is good, however, there is a setting where it is.

When to Set the Mood

If you and your partner are looking to start into something in the evening, do not wait until just before you hit the bedroom to set the mood. Use the entire day, even when you are at work. You can text your partner throughout the day little things that will get their motor running, and make them more ready and open to converse with you sexually.

When you are trying to set the mood, you can engage in dirty talk then, starting at a mild level, and then going up from there as the day transcends.

Getting in the Mood

How to Get Him in the Mood

Although your man could not take his hands off you when you first met, he might seem not in the mood after a while. He might get distracted once in a while and look somehow off, hence the need for you to get him in the mood. Despite the fact that most men easily get in the mood for sex, yours might seem a bit off on some days.

These tips should help you get him back in the mood for hot sexual sessions:

Prepare Him Bubble Bath

When your man comes back home from work after a long day's work, you can welcome him with a candle-lit bubble bath scented with vanilla. Various studies indicate that men get aroused the most by the smell of vanilla. You can take it a notch higher by waiting for him naked in the tab with two glasses of wine.

Give Him a Sensual Massage

You can give him a sensual massage to arouse his feelings and get him in the mood. Use things like fluffy wool or feathers or silky scarves to gently flip all over his body. Cinnamon scented candle and massage oils like frankincense and lavender are perfect for the sensual massage session. You can add more vigor to the massage by blindfolding your man.

Whisper Sexy Words in His Ears

When around him, whisper sexy words in his ears while letting him feel your deep breaths. You can also leave him a sexy voice message in your sexiest voice.

Look Him Directly in the Eyes

Enhance intimacy and arouse your man by staring directly into his eyes; do not blink or break your gaze. Well, don't just stare at him; use lustful eyes to lock your eyes with his and you will see how turned on he is. Men go crazy at the thought of a horny woman. If you could tell him that you are not wearing anything down there, his lust for you will go on overdrive.

Sing Him a Love Song

Choose one of your man's favorite love songs that you also like. Record yourself singing it and save it on a CD. Leave it on his car seat so he can find it in the morning as he leaves for work. When he gets to listen to it, he won't stop thinking about you throughout the day. He will be eager to come back home and share good intimate moments with you.

Express Your Feelings through Poetry

Write either a traditional or naughty poem about what you love about your man, your love life or even the first time you met. Leave it somewhere open where he will find it, or just read it to him. You can do the reading in bed.

Find the Way to His Heart

They say one of the ways to a man's heart is through good food. Prepare his favorite dish and place a sexy note next to the serving, letting him know your expectations of him later in the evening or night.

Give Him Flowers

According to a certain study conducted by the University of Rutgers, most men love receiving flowers, it increases their happiness and interactions socially. Choose his favorite colors or send him a bouquet of blue, red and purple flowers with the scents he loves most. Deliver the flowers with a sexy note.

Buy Him a Gift

Surprise your man with a gift you are sure he will love. You can also ask him to accompany you to a lingerie store and help you select something that he would love to see you wear.

Share a Bar of Chocolate

Studies associate chocolate with less depression and loneliness in men. You can also choose a menu that features chocolates to share with your man. There are several online that you can try.

Deep throat Him

Your man will definitely love the feeling of his penis deep in your throat. You can start by sucking his not erect penis until it is hard before you can deep-throat him. If this is something you cannot do, you can give him a visual effect by deep throating a toy penis.

Shave or Wax for Him

Men love the soft feel of smooth skin. Rub his penis gently against rough areas of your skin and slowly move to the smooth shaven or waxed areas so he can feel the difference in touch. You should do this firmly and lightly until he is so hard that he begs to feel the warmth of your vagina.

Nibble the Back of His Neck

Arouse the sexual desire in your man by nibbling the back of his neck using your tongue. Letting him feel your deep breaths is a plus.

Give Him a Spicy Kiss

Apply a spicy lipstick on your lips before kissing your man. It will spice up your oral sex sessions. He will get stimulated while you enjoy using your hot lips on him.

Rub His Penis

Gently hold your man's penis with your fingers and gently rub him. You can apply some lotion or gel to reduce friction and facilitate the arousal.

Get him to dress you

A horny man is a very creative one and will spend any amount of money to get his sexual fantasies met. Give your man a chance to dress you from head to toe for an entire week and see what happens. Let him do the shopping for the stuff that he wants you to wear. He will love it when you follow what he says. And the thought that you are wearing the clothes that he bought you will make him want you even the more. He will be looking forward for a wonderful session when he sees you.

Make the First Move

When you know he is about to get home, get naked and spread yourself on the bed waiting for him. His first sight of you will definitely arouse him and get him in the mood. You can also take the first step during other times, for instance, when you are relaxing in the living room over the weekend. You can move closer to him and start kissing him; he will definitely respond. Just ensure that he is in a good mood before making the move.

You can also undress him and push him onto the bed before you take charge and do the riding. You can also give him a quickie, look good for him, give him blowjobs, spank his butt, get him ready from the moment he wakes up, and stimulate his senses to get him in the mood.

How to Get Her In The Mood

According to two psychology professors at the Texas University and co-authors of the book 'Why Women Have Sex: Understanding Sexual Motivations from Adventure to Revenge', women need to be inspired in order to get in the mood for sex, whereas men are up for it anywhere and anytime, irrespective of the prevailing situation.

Men often wish that their women would respond more to their sexual gestures, or even initiate sex more. This difference is attributed to the fact that women's desire for sex depends on their immediate environment in terms of response and variance. Women experience sex in both their bodies and minds; men, on the other hand, focus more on their genitals.

Men are compared to firemen, who are ready to have sex anytime because to them, it is an emergency. Women, however, are exciting just like fire; the surrounding conditions must be right for them to fire up, let alone keep burning.

Your woman wants to have sex only when she thinks it is worth it. Therefore, you need to motivate your wife or girlfriend, for them to see sex as an exciting priority. Here are some ways to help you get her in the mood:

Give Her Mild Bondage

Your woman can be turned on by the mere thought that you are entirely responsible for her satisfaction sexually. You can get her ready by sending her an email or leaving a voice message or note earlier in the day. Tell her to put on some make up and wear your favorite outfit.

If you love a submissive woman, you can order her to submit to you by getting her on her knees and being your 'slave' just for the moment. Be her master and order her to do what you want. You can also use a gentle item to tie her as bondage and use a tickler or feather to arouse her.

You can also opt for gentle bondage sex toys or just spank her lightly using your hand. Note that the aim of the bondage is to bring your woman pleasure so that she can climax; no kind of pain or humiliation should be involved.

Role Play

You can ask her to role play her fantasy or be the slut you always yearn for. You can ask her to play the role of a stripper and give you one of a kind shows. If she is okay with having a camera around, you can decide to record the show for future use and reference.

Make Her Mind Sex

For women, sex starts in the mind. Your woman cannot think of having sex with you if she has other things occupying her mind. Tell her what you want to do to her in advance in detail. When together, rub your hands against her body and kiss her shoulders up her neck.

Remove her panties with her clothes on and slip your hand beneath her dress or top to tease her nipples. You can use the other hand to gently touch and rub her butt. You can let her arouse herself as you watch by rubbing her clit; let her sit on a chair with legs apart.

You can ask her to describe how she feels and before you know it, she will be begging you to do that to her, but with your hard penis deep inside her vagina.

Explore Her Fantasies

You can ask your woman to give you details of her sexual fantasies. By just sharing that kind of information with you, she will automatically get aroused. However, you need to prepare for the unexpected as her fantasy or what turns her on might make you insecure; there is no need for that.

Take advantage of that opportunity for your own gain. You can tell her story that matches her fantasy as you caress and kiss her gently. Whisper softly in her ears and let her imagination be her only limitation. If she responds to it, you can be sure that she is getting wet as well.

Watch Passionate Porn Together

Unlike men, women prefer aural porn. Find a suitable one with a sexy storyline and enjoy listening together. A passionate visual erotica would do though if you can find one. As you get aroused watching or listening to your favorite erotica, you can run your hands inside her clothes for greater arousal and pleasure.

Make Compliments

Women love compliments mainly because they are more self-conscious regarding their nude bodies and easily get insecure than their male counterparts. You need to make your woman feel secure in order to get her in the mood.

As you caress her body and give her hot kisses, tell her that you find her attractive, what you like most about her body, and how much she turns you on; and, you just can't keep your hands and tongue off her body. The more specific your compliments about her are the better.

You can tell her you love her soft skin, warm smile, beautiful shape or even size, and the soft feel of her firm breasts. Actually, the more you compliment her daily, the more she will always be in the mood.

Caress Her Sensually

You can easily get your woman in the mood by simply giving her tender strokes of your touches all over her body. As you touch her, your aim is to get her aroused for intercourse. Use long gentle caresses to massage her breasts and touch her all over. You can also move your hands down her body and put your hand in her panties to gently rub her clit.

Maintain the slow tempo throughout until she is totally aroused. Only then can you play rough, as she would be asking for.

Prolong the Foreplay

Foreplay means the world to women. Do not just rip off her panties and expect her to let you penetrate. You need to engage her in prolonged foreplay before you can make love to her. Hold her close, stroke her hair, touch her face, look directly into her eyes, kiss her soft spots, caress her body, and even kiss her neck.

You can also give her a sensual massage as part of foreplay to arouse her properly. The gentle touch of your fingertips all over her body, commonly known as 'spider legs' can get your woman really wet, ready for intercourse.

Create a Good Ambience

The right ambience to a woman is as good as being in the mood. You need to ensure that the ambience is stress-free, has proper lighting, is quiet, and if possible, smells great. The environment should also be clean because your woman will definitely love that.

It is easier for you to get her in the mood if the ambience is good because it relaxes and calms her mind to focus only on the feelings you are trying to arouse in her.

Rules of the Game

Rule 1: Welcome Back to Virginity

In every way that really matters, each couple setting out on The Sex Bucket List must be unadulterated, honest virgins!

Imagine (or grasp) that you are fresh out of the plastic new to the sex game.

You've never been given a climax You've never contacted your accomplice explicitly You've never at any point taken your accomplices garments off in the warmth of the minute That implies, you can't experience the rundown check off filthy things that you've just done… in light of the fact that recall that, you're authoritatively virgins (once more).

Rule 2: Take Turns Choosing your Sexy Challe

Ladies first, men second. The lady picks ANY provocative pail list challenge that turns her on and her accomplice must withstand. At that point, it's the man's turn.

Much the same as foreplay, you don't need to experience this sex container list in any specific request. Let your sex drive do the picking. At the point when an insidious opportunity

presents itself or you get a specific desire to play out a dream –
pull out all the stops.

Rule 3: "Game On"

Some Bucket List difficulties happen normally, similar to the
lady starting morning sex or the man twisting his woman over
in the shower. While others, like dream play or telephone sex,
can require some correspondence of what precisely is going to
occur.

At the point when it's your chance to pick a devious
demonstration that requires a common comprehension, and
you know precisely what you need, utilize the words "Game
On" to tell your accomplice that it's playtime.

These enchantment words signal that you're going to check off
a sex challenge, regardless of whether it pretends or areola
cinches. You can content this code to your accomplice on your
path home from work, you can murmur it in their ear as your
hand slides down their jeans or can pass these words over the
table on a bit of paper as you advance toward the restroom for
a few enthusiastic open sexes.

Rule 4: No Double Dipping on Challenges Marked with "xxx"

At the point when you see "xxx" by a Bucket List challenge, this implies there must be at any rate 1 hour between the consummation of one sex challenge and the picking of the following.

This, my companions, is called Delayed Sexual Gratification.

A portion of these difficulties are intended to leave you asking for additional. You are intended to replay that hot make-out meeting again and again in your mind at work. What's more, you should need to surge home just to tear your accomplice's garments off. Realizing that your better half is kicking the bucket to have you is absolutely precious.

Along these lines, practice a little discretion… it will make your climaxes 10x as solid.

Rule 5: Temporary Pass

Possibly the Queen isn't prepared to have her can play with today around evening time… or the Lord isn't prepared to have he can play with. Every challenger is permitted 3 transitory passes, where the picking accomplice must pick another challenge for the present. You can return to the skipped challenge at a later date.

Rule 6: Swap and Combine Challenges

On the off chance that there is a test that you two completely concur isn't something, you wish to seek after… like engaging in sexual relations in a parking area… at that point swap it. With what? A blend of 2 difficulties. For instance.

Engage in sexual relations on in a parking area Engage in sexual relations on the kitchen table Give him a penis massage Your new test could be to… give him a penis massage on the kitchen table.

Get it? You should finish an aggregate of 100 difficulties before the finish of the rundown.

No cheating and no skipping!

Rule 7: Push your Limits

Sexual edification lies directly outside of your sensual safe place. You're going to require a receptive outlook and an eagerness to be defenseless.

Obviously, having a trio is harrowing… but on the other hand, it's screwing great. Start moderate and stir your way up to the difficulties that push you the most. Play by an "On the off chance that you never attempt, you'll never know" mindset and simply go with it.

In the case of something feels awkward, chuckle about it together. Bond over it together.

On this note, a piggyback principle to #6 … you may just swap a sum of 4 challenges. Not 4 difficulties each, however 4 difficulties complete. In the case of something feels odd and awkward, tell your accomplice "Hello, this feels peculiar and awkward. Help me through this one". The general purpose is to develop together and push your breaking points together.

Follow along. Keep Pace.

The most ideal approach to monitor your Sex Bucket List Challenge is with 2 highlighters. At the point when you finish, check every erratic the rundown.

♦ Assign 1 highlighter as the "I need to do this once more" shading

♦ Assign 1 highlighter as "Not my top pick" action shading What's more, for those "Unsure yet I'm willing to attempt it once more"

♦ exercises, circle it and return to it once you've wrapped up the rundown.

Keep pace by doing, in any event, 4 difficulties for each week. The objective is to go into an exceptional sexual retreat with your accomplice

– not a periodic bare movement when you have time. Before the finish of the rundown, you'll have changed your ordinary workweek into an energizing, energy-filled sex fest.

At the end of the day, don't take a year to finish this rundown! You'll lose all energy.

The Sex Bucket List Pact

Your first test begins now.

Snatch every others' butts, investigate every others' eyes and state, "We will get unusual in any event 4 times each week until this rundown is done".

Let's assume it once again. Was that abnormal? Great. Things are going to get a ton more bizarre. Your first attractive experience begins now.

Keep in mind, you don't need to go all together. Let your moxie do the picking…

Part 1: Virgin Territory

Do you recollect past times worth remembering of waiting for foreplay? The days when you were all the while clutching your virginity and investigating your sexuality for hours one after another… over the garments? We're returning it to the rudiments.

1. Dry Hump–xxx

Try not to think little of how hot and hot this guiltless little bother can be.

Jump over your accomplice and start gradually kissing their neck and snacking on their ear while you gradually start to crush on their lap. This will advance into an all-out make out meeting with a hard chicken and wet undies.

The standard: no sex and nothing underneath the garments. You must leave like great little virgins.

2. Let Her Watch

Give yourself handwork while she watches. She isn't permitted to kiss you, to contact herself or to contact you. This is a limited show.

3. Let Him Watch

Lay back and satisfy yourself simply like you would alone. Do whatever it is that turns you on and let him figure out how you like to be contacted and what carries you to climax.

Same principles as above.

4. Make Out for 20 Minutes (Hands in Neutral Territory)- xxx

Rediscover what it feels like to kiss your band together with no closure objective. There is no race to detach every others' garments or convey the circumstance to the room.

Simply recollect what it feels like to truly want one another and speak with just your tongues.

5. Make Out for 15 Minutes(Touch Each Other Over the Clothes)- xxx

Kiss each other as enthusiastically as you'd like and let your hands cooperate.

Squeeze her areolas and snatch her can. Rub on that hard lump in his jeans and let him rub you through your underwear. What's more, much the same as in the past… leave. As the standards direct, you can finish a subsequent basin list challenge in one hour after you complete the process of making out.

6. Sext

Throughout the day. While you're both grinding away or school, send each other filthy messages specifying what you will do to one another once you get home.

7. Tease Your Partner with SexyPhotos #SendNudes

The two people are visual animals! Send your darling an attractive photograph of yourself in the exercise center storage space with those tight game bra titties or a photograph of all of you wet right out of the shower. It's everything about points!

8. Give Him a Hand Job

The way into decent handwork is bunches of lube, regardless of whether that be KY Lube, Coconut Oil or spit and salivation – get that infant wet. Request that your man appears you how he prefers it OR bothers him until he completely can't stand it any longer furthermore, is imploring you to make him cum.

The Rules: You can't utilize your mouth and he can't complete himself.

9. Make Her Cum with Just your hands

A lady's vagina resembles a mix lock; everyone requires an alternate code to get to the products. Discover that code!

Possibly she enjoys 2 fingers entering her or she may adore you just scouring her with your fingers. Work it out and don't be hesitant to animate her areolas with your free hand if that is the stuff to get her there.

10. Phone Sex

Anyplace, whenever. Call your accomplice while they are busy working and start speaking profanely or call them while they're at a social capacity and let them know what you're doing to your body at that point. To be clear with respect to what is going on… don't be reluctant to utilize the enchantment words – "Game On".

11. Cyber Sex

Whenever both of you are isolated, regardless of whether that be in various urban areas or in various rooms – compensate for the separation with a little digital bother.

Facetime or Skype as you contact one another, speaking profanely and portraying what you need to do to your sweetheart's body. Garments might be shed, toys may be utilized, and full-on climaxes might be had.

12. Titty Fuck

We should expect that you both are extra horny virgins with a creative mind, will we?

Folks, slide your chicken in the middle of those two excellent bosoms and delight yourself. Young ladies have a go at scouring your areolas simultaneously to truly get in the soul.

This game isn't only for Double D's! On the off chance that you don't have a tit valley to work with. Handwork while scouring the tip of his penis all over your areolas will work, as well. Keep in mind: lube is your companion.

13. Mutual Stimulation

The more turned on she is, the more love she places into that handwork. The more smoking his handwork is, the more enthusiastically those fingers are going to finger that wonderful pussy. Try not to squeeze each other to cum, simply appreciate the ride and see where it takes you.

14. Suck Toes

There are focuses on your feet and toes that are legitimately associated with your attractive spots. You'd be astounded how strongly a little blameless toe sucking can turn you on. Attempt this movement for 5 minutes. In case you're getting a charge out of it, keep going.

Attractive Tip: To flavor this one up, start with certain leggings or socks on his or her feet and gradually strip them off.

Part 2: Everything Oral

Oral in bed is acceptable, oral on the kitchen counter is far and away superior. Just by tweaking a couple of factors like the spot and the position, you can make a spic and span sexual experience for both of you.

15. Go Down on Her Until Orgasm

Eating a lady's pussy resembles an Olympic game. Each game takes practice also, commitment, much the same as a lady's stunning vagina. Making a lady cum with your tongue takes the perfect measure of weight, speed, and time. You may think you comprehend what your lady likes, yet it's a great opportunity to find a few new problem areas.

Lick her in new places and ask her what feels better. Does she need you to go higher? Quicker? Tune in to the manner in which she groans. Quiet may mean "switch things up". Focus on how her body reacts and you'll be capable to give her that full-body climax.

Ace Tip: Most men don't have the foggiest idea about this, however here and there a lady's failure to cum from her accomplice giving her cunnilingus is that we stress that we're taking excessively long or that our accomplice isn't getting a charge out of it. Along these lines, this test is particularly for the young ladies who are too sacrificial to even consider letting themselves lay back and appreciate. Realizing that you're not going to quit licking her until she cums will get her out of her head and into the occasion.

16. Give Him a Blow Job

Cumming from oral and cumming from sex are 2 entirely unexpected encounters. Treat your man to an unwinding and sexy BJ anyway you like it. Play with that chicken in new manners. Lick it, spit on it, slap it against your tongue, rub it all the rage. Truly make this blowie your own.

17. Ride His Face

There are two very hot approaches to ride your man's tongue. One: Sit all over and cover him with your entirely pussy. He'll adore it.

Try not to be reluctant to delicately ride him to and fro, giving his tongue a little bit of consolation. Even better, have something strong to clutch. This will give permit you more control.

Two Have him jump on his knees while you put one decisive advantage over the kitchen counter or work area. This will give him full access to all the enjoyment territories. He can likewise utilize his hands to move you exactly how he prefers.

18. Sixty-Nine

A man lying on his back, Woman straddling his face while his rooster is splendidly situated for her to play with.

Women, you can utilize your hands and your mouth here. Men of their word, you can utilize your hands to move her to and fro all over for a few additional incitements.

19. Blow Job Under the Table

While he's having his morning espresso at the table or in supper, nimbly slide under the table and unfasten his jeans. The rest is up to you what's more, your mouth. Have fun down there.

20. Sweet Cunnilingus

Chocolate Syrup, Ice Cream, Frosting – it's the ideal opportunity for dessert.

Here's the test: totally spread her quite pussy in the delectable treat of your decision. You're going to lick every last bit of it up until she comes. Try not to be hesitant to make a wreck. The best oral is constantly chaotic.

21. The Lollipop Blow Job

Prepared to get clingy?

Before you begin sucking on him, begin sucking on candy while you get him began with your other hand. Watching you lick that sucker will get him quickly hard. After you've prodded him enough, utilize the entirety of that extra spit and clingy squeeze in your mouth to give him the most delectable penis massage ever – simply don't put that candy down. Stop on occasion to suck a little more, spit a portion of those juices all over his rooster, and bother him while he asks for you to wrap up.

22. Blindfolded Blow Job

Utilize a tie or purchase a pleasant silk eye veil for your lady to give you a blindfolded head. Without her sight, she'll utilize every last bit of her different faculties to truly get into it as she feels and tastes her route all over your chicken.

23. No Moving Allowed

We as a whole need to cum! For the most part, when somebody is giving us orally, we are attempting to make ourselves cum. Be that as it may, the climaxes are so a lot more grounded when you simply let them occur. In this way, here's the standard: While you go down on your accomplice, they aren't permitted to move. Not their hands or their hips. Each time they move, you quit sucking or licking. They will be compelled to lay back and let that climax assume control over their whole body.

24. Lick His Nipples

Areola play isn't only for ladies. A few men have extremely delicate areolas that carry them to climax… and a few men don't. You'll never know until you attempt.

Lick with a delicate tongue, lick with a solid tongue, squeeze, and chomp. Attempt everything to perceive what works and what doesn't. Give it a couple of moments before you surrender.

25. Swallow

For a man, having the tip of his penis licked and sucked from the very starting as far as possible of a knock work is completely socks off blowing. Let him finish in your mouth and it will resemble the Christmas of oral sex.

Explore your Sexual Fantasies

Solo Fantasies

Let's start by saying that everyone has sexual fantasies. Many people feel ashamed of their turn on-s and inner erotic thoughts, but no matter what the fantasy is, it's completely normal.

There is but one place to start from: yourself. You will only find the peace of mind by knowing your own fantasies. Fantasy emerges from within you, and you have to use it like you mostly like. Some may be hot only as fantasy while masturbating. Others might be things you want to test out for real.

Masturbation - Do it

Mostly all people masturbates, and although our emotions about it range from embarrassment to confidence and our masturbation sessions vary from robotic to laid back, we all share one aspect, we all believe in one thing: masturbating is healthy.

Many Volumes about the health benefits arising from masturbation have been published, refuting outdated misconceptions that have discouraged people from feeling better about this healthy activity. Masturbation is a relief opportunity for some individuals. Masturbation is known as something soothing, satisfying, and pleasant in all its ways. We do something positive to ourselves when we masturbate, by taking nutrients and blood into our penis or vagina and strengthening our pelvic muscles by holding them strong and healthy. And also we can say, simple and straightforward, that it feels damn good.

Masturbation is where everything starts for us physically, from our first orgasms to our first experiences, and can influence all the rest of our sexual activities. If we want to try something new, like vibrators, or an original sex method, and so on, masturbation is the most reliable tool to help us out discover.

The imagination drives our sessions of masturbation.

In fact, even if our stimulation is solely physical, a warm fantasy may support it, and make it better.

Combined pleasure, stimulation, and imagination can be an active learning tool to achieve:

- Faster and more intense, efficient orgasm.

- Orgasm during sexual relationship, such as oral sex, anal sex, or The full intercourse.

- Overcoming of sexual apprehension and discomfort, such as intimacy with a new partner, shyness, tension, nervousness of trying new things.

Also, you can adjust your sexual habits; for instance, while masturbating, you can try to approach to new sensations such as anal sex or mild discomfort (BSDM), and you can freely increase or decrease in intensity depending on

your needs.

Fun Masturbation Sessions: Fantasies, Sex Toys, and More

Once you have known your dream, you just need to focus on it, and find out how you can make it more accurate and comfortable. Be a little predictive; perhaps you might need a shopping journey or two to buy some accessories before to start.

Public Masturbation

It's more than common news to hear that some people like to masturbate in public. And this is something especially done by man. Why? Psychologists formulate that the public display of genitals or masturbation is an exhibitionist disorder. Jilted lovers seeking revenge seem to find pleasure forcefully masturbating in front of women. The look of fear and humiliation on the women's face appeals to them. Men do not do it because they want the woman/women; it's because they hate them, and this is a really regressive thought to have. Much of this behavior also finds its roots in the past abuse, whether emotional or physical.

So if you think masturbating in public is one of your hidden fantasies, you should start to scan yourself and find out why you actually like it. Could it be related to psychological distress? Or excite you knowing you could get caught?

If you select the first option, you should seriously consider seeing a specialist. This leads to nothing good, and you may even be imprisoned if caught engaging in obscene acts in a public place.

Unfortunately, even the second option doesn't allow you to masturbate in public, you will need to find a different way to satisfy your excitement for the danger, and the prohibited, your desire for transgression.

It is imperative that when masturbating, you need to make sure nobody is going to see you unless you find someone will be watching you. Even if it could be part of the thrill for the danger, when someone sees you, it's not all right, as you engage him or her in a sexual act without his or her permission for it.

Established that you better stay in your room, we have to say that this doesn't mean you can't indulge in your little fantasies, with the aid of pornographic videos and images in porn books and magazines. In this way, you could physically fall into the scene that must arouse you, as you masturbate into orgasm.

You can imagine yourself being anywhere you like, even in a place prohibited in real life. Furthermore, you can actually become what you see: that cock in the mouth, or the man who penetrates, or you can be that pussy being licked or penetrated.

Explicit Images

Having some explicit images in front of you while masturbate will definitely improve your experience.

Especially for some people who may not have enough imagination, or maybe inclined to be distracted by their own thoughts.

Many people, therefore, make use of porn movies or erotic images. Or even there are people who use live video, sex chat, etc.

People who are faithful in their love affairs may use their partners for an exchange of erotic messages and dirty photos.

In short, the options are so many, but one that you may have never considered is self-mirroring. Mirrors can bring pornographic images at the next point for someone who has never seen him/herself near and sexually stimulated, being in front of a mirror can be a very interesting experience. You may provide your sights with a well-placed mirror, by gazing at your whole body and genitals while you masturbate. You may have a little mirror in your room to bring closer to you, or you may just sit on the floor in front of a large mirror and play in different positions. It's twice as hot when you see every step your hand makes to rub and drizzle yourself —and don't be afraid to even talk dirty if you like it.

To make the dream more vivid is better, you don't use porn at the same time, as it could be distracting. Try, therefore, to only use the best arousing picture that you have in your heart and mind already!

Fantasies

If you rather not to watch anything, either yourself in the mirror, you can indulge in other fantasies with the only aid of your mind and why not some sex toys.

In fact, sex toys are not only great tools to masturbate, but they are also a great ingredient for your creative situations. You can imagine not be on your own, and receive anal sex, oral sex or hand free masturbation, as they can be replicated using several sex toys and appliances. Would a dildo in your mouth maybe render your group sex dream possible? Or would you be a prisoner of an erotic dungeon with the use of a nipple clamp?

Here are a few fancy sex items and ideas:

Masturbation sleeves bring the normal one-or two-handed movement to a whole new level of feeling. Sleeves come in a variety of forms, such as sizes, thicknesses, textures, and shades —and you can just pick the one you consider most appealing. With their help, you can better imagine to enter in a real ass or vagina.

If your dream is more about tits sex, your next session might be enriched by semi-real shaped breasts...

So if you are a man, you might like to rub your penis between your two breasts as you please; or just simply touch the breast and suck the nipples while masturbating.

Or maybe you are a woman with a hidden fantasy for other women, and you might like to stroke and stimulate your vagina on the swollen nipple, or again just play a bit with the breast while masturbating.

Dildos, as we said earlier, are non-vibrating phallic sex toys used for stimulation, and they can be used in a wide variety of fantasy scenarios. Everyone "required" to suck a dick could roll the dildo across his face and drive it into their mouth again and again, and while holding the dildo with one hand, keep masturbating with the other. Every fellatio dream can be enhanced by the dildo, and if you fancy some team sex, having multiple dildos can make the experience even more enjoyable. Also, you can put a dildo in a belt and start masturbating both the dildo and yourself. Obviously, everything will be boosted even more by the use of vibrating toys. Masturbation with a dildo, combined with fantasy, can be a very pleasurable experience, and especially for women, is an excellent way of learning how to orgasm from penetration, which most of the time is not so obvious.

Maybe your fantasy is more about sensations games relevant to your pleasure/pain desires.

If what turns you on is a bit of pain, you might like to start using some clamps.

Brief clamps and clips can easily be added to improve pinnacle emotions, but note that when you pull them off, they hurt a lot more because the blood rushes back to the already clamped region. You can use clamps on fleshy parts of your body like breasts, boobs, stomach, legs, hips, penile skin and testicles, and lips and lumps! Place them in line with your fantasy situation, but don't keep them on longer than your masturbation time. Such articles can be purchased in a sex toy or BDSM department. Check them before you shop with the soft flesh of your leg–they can be deceiving and can sting worse than it seems.

Also, you can try things like mental bondage. Such as, tell yourself that no matter what, you can't move your legs (or whatever other parts of your body, or even tell yourself that you can't make any noises like moans), or there's going to be a punishment, such as a spanking.

Spanking is a pretty low risk activity, as long as you make sure you're not hitting anything that you can easily damage (kidneys, tailbone, hips, spine, neck, face, ears), and you can do it to yourself. For things like wax play, make sure you're getting candles/wax that burns at low temperatures.

Also, Larger devices (dildo, vibrators, butt plugs, etc.), properly used, can make you feel more "violated," and any manipulating tool may be used to strengthen the illusion of being under someone else power.

Please be very careful when playing alone with discomfort, servility, fire, asphyxiation, or any dangerous game that causes pain.

Asphyxiation, for example, is very dangerous to try, although it is not rare as a fantasy, and can often be deadly. The electric play leaves plenty of room for a lethal mistake, so it should be made solely by electricity professionals and studied by a BDSM professional. When floating, it isn't at all advised to bind yourself (handcuffs, ties, restraints, silk scarves, etc.). Do not bind your hands or arms, though, and make sure that you can untie anything that you use to bind your legs/feet quickly. Blindfolding yourself shouldn't be that dangerous either, as long as you're sure you're in a safe place and, again, can easily take it off, so make sure that what you use it's not made of any silk-like material that will tighten when pulled.

What to Stick in Your Ass

What if you don't have any anal toys available at the moment, but you can't resist putting something up your ass?

You have undoubtedly heard urban legends about people going to the ER with all sorts of strange or potentially lethal things in their rectum— and sadly, many of them do it for real. Don't be hasty in choosing a random item; take the right judgment while rubbing your ass. Your anal sphincter pulling takes everything inside. Do not place in your ass anything which has sharp edges, can crack, move, smash, or not have a larger basis for easy removing.

You might need to wait until you can buy the right toy, as carrots are wrong! If you can't pull it back securely, you will take part in your urban legend.

Get the right tool for your work, like a butt plug or a discreet dildo for anal usage, and always use a lot of lubrication.

Someone may like to pleasure themselves from their own hands and not take the "risk;" however, proper anal devices make anal sex dreams more sensational. Anal beads can be added one at a time, left in or taken, gradually or quickly based on your desires. Alternatively, you can use a large butt plug that can be left in place during another operation to satisfy several fantasies, such as the possession or bondage...

Change Your Habits and Teach yourself new Skills

Once you have gained a deep intimacy with yourself, have explored all your fantasies, and the sensations they bring to you, you are ready to revolutionize your sex life.

Your amateur skills will only get better and better.

The first important thing to make a change in your relationship, as we have said and reiterated, is communication.

Now you know who you are, what you love, what you want, and what you can do. You can reveal to your partner all your wishes and fantasies.

And you can urge your half to share even their most intimate desires with you. But remember, your partner may need some alone time to discover oneself, too. At that point you can suggest that they try the same experiences as you, you can explain everything you have done to find the real you, and come back to you at the right time.

Once you know everything about each other, what is left to do is to find compromises on what can be integrated into your bed.

It is understandable that not everything is allowed, but it is important to make every effort to meet the needs of your partner.

In fact, sometimes romantic partners may disagree on when to have sex, how often to have it, where to have it, and what those sexual activities involve.

However, changing sexual habits (or making sexual transformations) for a partner can benefit the relationship. This is either because of the change itself that obviously give more pleasure to the partner either because people sense their partner's efforts to meet their sexual needs, and feel more relationship satisfaction because their partner is making those efforts.

You can start with the simplest things, and as your bond and understanding increase and your skills improve, you can move on to the next level.

By implementing everything gradually, with complicity, maintaining respect for each other, and above all, by loving and seeking the pleasure of the other, success is guaranteed!

Fantasies for Couples

Would you like to become the most desired sex toy of his or her own?

Fantasies are packed of suspense, excitement, risk, happiness, and love.

Specific dream possibilities come in infinite variations. I suggest that you use your imagination to decide what will work best for you— you don't use your intellect. Combine fantasy elements that both trigger and tend to combine: a sex act, a piece of clothing, a location, a difficulty, etc.

Here are some tips for launching you. You may draw up your favorite lists of things that you both would like to do, things you might like to use or wear, and places where to do it. You and your partner can select "yes," "no," or "maybe" next to each line to get a clear idea of what you both would want to be playing with.

Here below an example of what you could add to your list:

Masturbation, the mouth ejaculation, female ejaculation, genital penetration, sex with pants on, threesomes, two men, two women, many couples, male receptive anal penetration, female receptive anal penetration, watching porn, different roles.

Sex toys, lingerie, men's clothes, neckties, briefs jumper, pants, boots, shoes, socks, fabric, elastic, latex, cotton, bandages, neck, wedges, linen, ribbons, bows in the head, pigtails, bottles, skirts, formal dresses, tiaras.

Household places (Bedroom, living room, kitchens, offices, stairs, closets, garden, showers, and toilets), vehicles, workshop, bike, barns, woodsheds, lake, sex party, and poolside, deserted beaches, deserted forest, restaurants or bars or pubs toilet, car park.

Once the list is ready, you can find all the possible combinations, and the fun begins! We will now consider some of the most common fantasies and role games ideas, one by one.

1. Boss/employee

Fifty-six percent of women and 61 percent of men have sex fantasies about getting it on with co-workers in their office. So why not dress up in your work attire, get behind the desk, and re-create the hot new hookup scenario that's been on your mind? <u>The allure of having sex</u> with a coworker, especially your boss, has to do with gaining power.

2. Ravishment

According to a study from UCLA, 64 percent of women fantasize about this passionate and forceful kind of love. Why? Researchers felt that by imagining the man telling her what to do, the woman is able to give herself "permission to do the raunchy, hot sex stuff she feels a little embarrassed about, but deep down really does want to try."

This is different than the *rape fantasy*, which has often been misrepresented.

Of course, women don't want to be raped. Rape is an act of violence and power, not one of love. However, as revealed in romance novels, the fantasy of a strong, powerful man initiating sex with a woman, not accepting her initial reluctance, and then loving her passionately, is a highly popular fantasy.

Do the Fifty Shades Of Grey frenzy make more sense to you now?

3. Storybook lover

This fantasy is more based on love that can be found in romance novels than the kind that takes place in the Victorian era. Or it could really be any kind of book, even comics. Does any ever fancied to have sex with a superhero?

4. Exhibitionism

<u>In his study of sexual fantasy</u>, *Who's Been Sleeping in Your Head?* Brett Kahr found that 19 percent of people fantasize about being watched during sex, and another 5 percent fantasize about taking it off in public. In for the risk?
Put on a show. Get it on near the windows in your home or hotel room.

5. Voyeurism

Does watching the show from the sidelines turn you on?

Whether you're spying on the neighbors or the couple getting it on at the beach, this fantasy is a common one. One easy way to make it happen? Go to a nude beach or a sex show with your partner.

6. Mutual masturbation

Put a twist on your voyeuristic fantasy by watching your partner masturbate, or letting them watch you. It will help them understand more of what you desire, and of course, it's an instant turn-on.

7. The stranger fantasy

Getting comfortable is one of the pleasures of being in a long-term relationship: not having to put up a first-date front, getting takeout and watching TV, being boring together. It's a relief not to have to be "on" — to feel free to be in an unattractive mood or display one of your weird neuroses without worrying the other person will finally realize the truth about you.

But this is also a hazard of relationships: You can take your partner for granted and quit trying to impress. Couples forget how to flirt, or that they're attractive to anyone else, and get bored — with each other, and themselves.

- There's something _sexy_ and mysterious about anonymity.

- For as long as you've known your partner, pretend you don't.

- Different clothes, new hairstyles, different personalities, different names.

- Start by meeting at the bar and then take your new friend home.

- Keep in character the entire time.

Give in to this fantasy doesn't mean that you desire someone else, is more like going back on time when you first met, but this is going to be hard to play if not pretending to don't know each other first.

8. Make a sex video

A Stanford University study found that women reach peak arousal after just two minutes into an erotic flick. According to *Men's Health*, it's not just celebrities who want to make sex tapes — 40 percent of women want to make a homemade flick with their partners. So get on it while it's hot. After you watch it, make sure to hide it safely or quickly delete it.

9. Threesome

A LELO study revealed that 20 percent of women have had a threesome. Some say they love the rush and added stimuli, whereas others worry about jealousy and feeling overwhelmed. Talk it over with your partner to see if it's right for you.

To be honest, I don't recommend threesomes for couples in committed relationships. I'm all for them for people in casual, non-committed relationships, or 'situationships.' So if you are will to do so, you need to know why. If the threesome idea was sparked by boredom in the bedroom, bringing a new person into the mix disincentives you from putting energy and creativity into your sex life with your partner. It does not solve the longer- term issue of how to keep things fresh and become a better lover. When it comes to picking a third, many couples gravitate to someone they know. This is a huge mistake. Inviting someone into the bedroom, which one or both of you already have an emotional bond with, makes it more likely that someone will have feelings or someone will get their feelings hurt.

Picking up strangers at bars can also be tricky. Fortunately, there are many apps, like Tinder and Feeld, designed specifically to help you out. Once you both agree on a potential partner, I recommend meeting him/her for a "date" before inviting him/her straight to bed, so you can make sure the photo is real, test the chemistry, and see how it feels to take the next step. If you do feel comfortable moving forward, there are other safety measures to consider. First up: Birth control. Make sure that if someone is wearing a condom, he does not double-dip. Check that everyone involved has a clean bill of health and establish in advance with your partner whether there will be any exchanging of bodily fluids. Limiting drugs and alcohol prevent things from getting out of control and makes it easier for everyone to keep their agreements.

Certainly not everyone's fantasy, but if you enjoy threesomes and are curious about bringing more partners into the bedroom, group sex might be one of the more thrilling and liberating fantasy to explore.

10. Public sex

According to *Men's Health*, 64 percent of women want to step outside the bedroom and get frisky in public. It makes sense — the rush, risk of getting caught — and it all adds to your experience. Talk about where you both feel comfortable doing the deed, whether it's an elevator or bathroom.

11. Outdoor sex

Want the thrill of getting it on outside the bedroom but want to decrease your chances of actually getting caught? Embrace the elements and try doing it in a secluded area outside at night. The grass, the sand, the pool, the great outdoors is your sex playground.

12. Airplane sex

Been there, done that with the whole public sex thing? Take it to the next level by joining the mile-high club. According to *Men's Health*, 51 percent of women want to get it on up in the air. Take off!

If you try to imagine how you'd have airplane sex on a commercial flight, the obvious way would be to go to the bathroom. After all, an airplane is a public place, and no one should have to witness people having sex, so usually, the lavatory is your only option. My whole take on it is, as long as you aren't doing it in public, you're quiet about it, and you haven't been acting suspicious the entire flight, if you want to go have sex in the lavatory, then have it. It's certainly not high on the list of places I'd want to have sex, especially given that the lavatory is cramped, smelly, and the liquid on the floor isn't water... But to each their own.

13. Using sex toys

According to the LELO survey, 76 percent of women want to use their toys with their partners. And ladies, don't be embarrassed to ask about unleashing the toys. The survey found that 89 percent of men would be happy to use them. And it's not just for your benefit? Sixty-eight percent of couples both climax during intercourse with sex toys.

14. Visit the strip club

Thought the nudie bar was dudes-only? Think again. According to Men's Health, 47 percent of women want to visit a strip club with their guy. It's exciting, sexy, and you'll be there together. The strip club just has a way of bringing out your inner god. Maybe it's the lights, maybe it's the alcohol, or maybe it's the fact that you see a dancer twerking like you never thought possible. Strip clubs may have a bad reputation for glamorizing and catering to the more base desires of men, but as we said, they're also frequented by women — and a lot of these clubs are very high-end. There's a certain ambiance that could inspire you to bring out your inner sex kitten.

A lot of women may feel intimidated and uncomfortable with the numerous amounts of bare breasts parading in front of their man.

But keep in mind that the dancers are there for a job and not to hook up with your significant other. Just because a dancer approaches him doesn't mean he's thinking about leaving you or fantasizing about her. Let the jealousy stay at home and enjoy the moment.

Not sure if it's your thing? Find one with a twist, like the Vegan strip club in Portland. Lap dance for two, please.

15. Domination

Power is a rush, there's no doubt about it.

Not to win, but to surrender! The mere thought of a partner sweeping them off their feet and winning full sexual control over them provides a heady adrenaline rush. Women just love watching their macho lover begging for sexual release in the bedroom as they crack the whip on their love slave. And hot hunks also get turned on by the thought of being hand-cuffed in bed as their lady love assumes the role of the dominating lover. Many women dream about having a man obey their every wish, so why not unleash your
inner dominatrix and try it out in the bedroom? You'll be in total control and he'll be completely devoted. You can simply just tie your partner's limbs to the bed, and there's your prey all set to submit to your sexual calls. He's the slave and you the master.

So go ahead and live out your carnal pleasures. Touch, tease and tickle, the situation is a win-win at both ends. Your slave is bound to derive pleasure in begging for your sexual attention, as you enjoy making him deliver your hidden whim and fancies!

16. Submission

Many <u>women also fantasize about being submissive</u> and losing control to their partner.

In <u>2009, the University of Kansas study</u>, it was discovered that "forceful submission fantasies" aren't about humiliation but are instead "a passionate exchange with a powerful, resource-holding and attentive suitor." So you can also decide on taking turns to those who submit and who dominate.

17. Teacher/student

There's a reason "<u>Hit Me Baby One More Time</u>" was such a popular music video, and we're going to guess it wasn't because of <u>Britney Spears</u>' vocal chords. The schoolgirl fantasy can involve dominance and spanking, but it doesn't have to. For some, it's just sexy outfit to rip off.

The professor-and-student scenario is relatively easy to improvise because both characters have clear goals: The Student wants the grade, and the Professor wants the Student. Both roles can take the initiative and play into their parts without any confusion about where the scene is going.

This kind of scenario is popular as it gives a chance to safely play with power dynamics — but you can switch up how you do it. For example, you think the teacher has power and the student doesn't; however, that doesn't have to be the case. You can have a student who's blackmailing the teacher, who's seducing the teacher, who's doing the teacher a favor, who's soothing the teacher because they're having marriage problems.

18. Knight in shining armor

Romantic? This is a fantasy for you. Whether he's a fireman saving you from a smoky room, or a lifeguard carrying you out from the ocean, in this fantasy, your guy comes to your rescue and then seduces you.

19. Put on a strip show

Guys will surely love this one. But for the ladies, it's just as enjoyable. You get to put on your sexiest lingerie, take it off and tease him/her in the process, private lap dance included. The dancer will have control and the partner will be turned on and begging for more.

20. Use food

Food and sex have a lot in common — they're sensual, nourishing, and have the potential for great variety.

One of the easiest, most delicious ways to literally spice up your sex life is by combining sex with food and adding some edible ingredients to your bedroom routine.

In fact, "food play" is especially suited to long-term relationships.

Hopefully, you and your partner already know each other's tastes and preferences, as well as how to communicate what you do and don't like. Whether using food on the tongue or body (more on this later), food foreplay is an appetizer, but sex is the meal. So hold the savory and spicy (which can burn skin or eyes), and stick to sweets for your sweet.

If you're into healthier sweets, try pieces of fresh seasonal fruit, like cherries, strawberries or mango slices. If you're more of a candy craver, play with ice cream toppings, like caramel sauce or marshmallow crème. Or go crazy and combine the two! You can gently hand feed each other, licking and sucking fingers or use each other's bodies as plates gently nibbling the food from it.

Just remember that a little goes a long way. Eating too much before getting intimate will only make you and your partner feel sluggish, give you a sugar crash later, and may even lead to motion sickness.

Private parts and food don't mix for various reasons, including the potential for infections, skin irritation, and let's be real, sticky pubic hair. If you're using plain ice, feel free to explore all over. Otherwise, the safest way to stimulate your partner is to keep all the food action above the waist. But don't worry: there are plenty of erogenous safe zones.

To keep things hot, try foods you can heat up, like chocolate or honey. Or you can go in the opposite direction with popsicles, frozen grapes, or just plain ice. Play around with these items, hot and cold alike, running them over sensitive zones.

21. Uniforms

Love a man in uniform? For some, it's the clothes, and for others, it's their courage. According to psychologist and relationship experts, the 'uniform' may signify that the man is able to manage life's troubles.

Uniforms—military in particular—are sexy because they connote discipline, composure, competence, achievement, and intelligence. However, this is not only a female fantasy. These are all highly desirable traits from everyone.

So what are you waiting for? Have your partner dress the

part and play the role?

22. Play doctor

Sick and the only way to fully recover is with an orgasm? Doctor to the rescue.

Medical fantasies may be based on erotic feelings or thoughts you had during past experiences or be inspired by sexy characters you've seen in movies or television. Maybe you want to be patient being examined and cared for, the skillful doctor who knows just what the patient needs or the naughty nurse who knows how to make everything feel better. You may even have a fetish for the type of outfit, medical equipment used (latex gloves, speculum, rectal thermometer, stethoscope, stirrups, etc.) or a particular procedure.

Dress in an official looking outfit or get a sexy costume for the job. Wear glasses and use a clipboard to look more the part. You can even snap on a pair of latex gloves for effect. Bring along a bag of sex toys and other accessories to use as pretend medical devices.

Start off by asking your patient some intimate questions as you feel around their body. Ask to undress then run a complete set of sensitivity and sexual performance tests.

After your probing exam, you'll be able to give your expert diagnosis: More Sex Required! You can then write your patient a sex note detailing exactly what you want them to do. Of course, you'll want a few follow-up visits and, with your bedside manner, they're sure to come often.

There are lots of possible erotic variations in these types of sexy medical scenarios – different characters, settings and situations can all be combined to make your role play games even more thrilling.

- Here are a few ideas to inspire your erotic imagination:

- You're a patient getting a free procedure in exchange for being observed by a group of medical students. A video camera is also being used to record the session and give everyone closes up details.

- You're a sex researcher hunting for proof that the mythical G-Spot exists so you can unlock its orgasmic potential. After a detailed exam and warm-up experiments, use your elegant, specially designed g-spot detector devices to gather evidence of your discover.

- You're a patient in a full-body cast that has a few convenient openings. It's been months since you've had sex and there's an itch that only your naughty nurse can relieve.

- You're a medical student looking for extra credit, so you volunteer for a sex research program. The researcher tests observe and measure your sexual response during masturbation and intercourse using a variety of devices.

- You're experiencing sexual dysfunction and have resorted to an unconventional treatment program using exotic electro-stimulation devices and other pain/pleasure instruments.

- You're an unethical/unconventional doctor who believes in sexual therapy to cure almost every ailment. Use your authority to order what you want or use other means to administer your special therapy personally.

- You're a nurse at a sperm bank with a special incentive to meet your quota. Some clients tend to be shy and need a little assistance producing their deposit, but you have ways to get the job done with very satisfying results.

23. Act out your favorite sex scene from a movie

Get into character and re-create your favorite cinematic sex scene. Whether it's Basic Instinct or a celebrity sex tape, discuss the scene with your partner and get ready for an Award-winning Academy performance.

24. Sensual massage

You can play a role play between a sexy massage therapist and the client.

Unleash your imagination to reconstruct the right environment as similar to a luxurious massage center. And use what you learned about sensual massage in previous chapters. Get with it and make your partner melt with an arousing rub down.

Or what you prefer is perhaps a real couple massage in a specialized center. Ever heard of a happy ending massage?

You can find one that offers this type of service, or you can enjoy yourself right after the massage in the dressing room, either having sex together, If possible or, masturbating thinking of each other.

24. Erotic spanking

Why do people love kinky butt-smacking? Aside from physical pleasure, people love erotic spanking for the taboo thrill of it.

There is an ENORMOUS difference between spanking and erotic spanking.

One makes you want to sprint away like an Olympic contender and call social services. The other makes you want to run towards the bedroom and scream that you've been a bad little boy/girl.

They can hurt like hell (and often leave marks behind), so why do we savor the sensation? The answer is simple.

When we're stressed or in pain, our brains release A LOT of chemicals. One of the key players is dopamine, which is present in the body during pain AND pleasure. Many agree this might be one of the reasons we can combine pain and pleasure in a single situation.

The act of spanking can add another element of pleasure because the posterior is plentiful with nerves *and* right next door to the genitals. Strikes and slaps send waves and ripples through the skin and stimulate this fun area.

Whether you do this *carefully* or *bluntly* depends entirely on you and your significant other. No matter what kind of kink you are into, you should have a safe word.

Why? When we are role-playing, sometimes "No," "Don't," or "Stop" are part of the fantasy. However, if someone yells "PINEAPPLE!" it's a very clear signal that play needs to stop.

If you're not sure what word to choose, it can be anything that you normally wouldn't say, something easy to remember that pulls people out of the elation and makes them re-focus.

25. Personal trainer

Hate working out? Here's a way to enjoy it. One of you is the personal trainer, and the other is the obedient trainee.

26. Hot mechanic

Is hooking up with a shirtless hottie covered in grease your sexiest fantasy?

Here is another fancy role play for you! This scenario may take place on the seat of your car or maybe in the garage.

Have all the tools needed and use the lube instead of mechanical grease. I leave the rest all to your imagination.

27. Boat sex

Want to get it on out in the middle of the ocean? Well, I'm guessing you're a Di Caprio fan.

But even if you're not on a Titanic-like ship or a *Wolf Of Wall Street* yacht, there's still an opportunity to get down and dirty when you set sail.

And you're not the only one with the nautical fantasy. Match.com's Singles In America survey revealed that 50 percent of singles hope to have sex on boats.

You can make this a simple romantic sexual experience on the boat or spice it up with some role play game.

28. Feathers

Feathers ticklers are products that aid in sensory awakening.

Although these kinds of products fall into the category of bondage, have the ability to enhance the foreplay in the bedroom and not as intimidating as BDSM or bondage.

There are many couples out there that benefit the electrifying feeling they can achieve together using these simple but effective products. They are extremely easy to use and not very expensive, so everyone can consider using them as part of their bedroom antics. The feather tickler is made from several feathers that are collected together and bound together in a handgrip, from head to toe.

The idea of a feather tickler is to stimulate the sensory system, heighten the feeling across your erogenous zones and enhance the full-body experience by increasing the blood flow to the surface of the skin. The feather tickler is not complicated to use and can be the perfect aid in any sexual experience and a great way to explore the senses together with your loved one. You might even find it adds a little fun and laughter into the mix.

How do you use a feather tickler?

Well, take hold of the grip and use the tip of the feathers to softly stroke across your partner's body parts, starting at the less erogenous and slowly teasing more and more until you see them react. They will tingle from their head to their toes; you'll see goose pimples all over their body whilst they enjoy the feeling of their skin becoming more and more sensitive.

Try and experiment with different combinations of delicate strokes and longer harder strokes to see what works for your partner best. You'll begin to notice what is working and what's not. By doing this, you'll control the 'ups' and 'downs' of their heightened pleasure, teasing and tantalizing them in the buildup of your foreplay session.

Whether you choose to be tied up or not, have your partner tease you with the light touch of a feather.

To set the mood and enhance the experience, you may also benefit from adding other elements to the mix.

You might think of combining an eye mask or blindfold. Adding a blindfold, you'll notice that by taking one of the senses out of the equation, the other senses are heightened. A blindfold or eye mask will enhance stroke ever, making it more exciting and stimulating. Your ultimate goal is to increase your partner's exhilaration and provide an unimaginable ecstasy.

Also, with the addition of restraints, you'll stay in control by stopping your partner from escaping the teasing. Just enjoy watching your partner wriggle around, begging for you to stop.

29. Pegging

For those who aren't familiar, pegging is where a person with a vulva has anal sex with a partner using a strap-on, and —for those who are game— it can be a surefire way to flip the script on vanilla sex. Pegging plays with power dynamics and allows both partners to explore a different side of their sexuality. It's not for everyone, but if you're intrigued, talk to your partner to see if it is down with this type of get-down.

30. Hotel maid

Maybe it's the allure of being on vacation, but hotel sex is exciting and liberating, which may be why the maid fantasy is a hot one. Can't make it to the hotel? With a sexy maid costume and knock from "housekeeping," you can re-ignite the spark in no time, anywhere.

Fiction, or in reality?

How possible is it to you to create your dream?

When it comes to fantasy playing in your marriage, you have many choices. However, successful fantasy games need to take careful account of the situation, the pacing, and the physical and emotional comfort.

For every fantasy that you make, accept both comfort and security criteria, and mutually determine how far you want to push the creativity. The treat under his clothes may be sweet, but it might jeopardize his urinal behavior — or make his stall all day and feel uncomfortable rather than attractive.

Whether this is a light-hearted sex game or the unveiling of your most dark erotic dreams, communication will bring you closer. Your willingness to try (or at least discuss) new things gives rise to optimism. Our imaginations emerge from our deepest parts. We welcome someone else into our most private world once we reveal them. You will figure out the most erotic secret desires of each other and also the discomfort or the fears of each other. Like excited teenagers on their first day, you are on a sexual adventure that takes you far away from your old sexual routines.

You have to trust your partner to refrain from assessing your skill, quality, and even more scarce imagination.

Another important thing is to determine the boundary between fiction and reality. Only imagination implies you don't want to see them to be put into effect for real.

Many role plays will need to act out in a fictitious place.

You can't play the doctor in a hospital, or teacher and student in a school, etc. Also, acting to be a stranger doesn't mean that you would like to stay with a real stranger. Or like we said, for example, ravishment is not a real rape.

Domination and Submission are not made because you really want to hurt or get hurt.

Up to play? Are you armed for play?

You are suitable at playing now! Fantasies of natural sex acts can be performed when you're ready and wherever you want, with specific scenarios. Home is the perfect place to play your game, so partners will meet you with a little fancy talk and creativity to change the time and location as you want, and you are free to use costumes, sex toys, fetish, and accessories for some extra enjoyment.

Now just pick your first game and enjoy!

Ways To Make You Last Longer In Bed

So, this is more of a recap with a few new ideas thrown in for good measure. At the end of the day, most men want to be able to last longer in bed, not just those who suffer from premature ejaculation. We all know it isn't any fun for either of you when things end too quickly but, on the other hand, all the media hype that says you should be going at it for half an hour or more is also wrong. Many men are conscious of the fact that they may be finishing just a little too quickly for their partner as all those Hollywood movies and magazines would have you believe women love sessions that go on for hours.

That is all complete and utter rubbish and nothing but hype. That said, there are times when you could do with lasting just a little longer than a few minutes so here are some killer tips to help you hold back for longer:

1.   Back to your teenage years

Remember how, as a teenager, you used to spend what felt like hours kissing and making out without actually having sex? Felt good, didn't it. So, go back to doing that. Spend more time on kissing your partner, on exploring each other using your hands and your mouth before you even think about actually having sex.

2.   Learn how to massage

When you lead a busy life, it becomes quite difficult to find the time for sex and it isn't easy to make the move from your busy working life to a sexy erotic one. Stress is the culprit here and before you can even begin to feel like getting down to it, you need to de-stress. The very best way to do that is through massage, and if you do it properly, both you and your partner will be completely turned on by it. You do need to learn how to do this properly, though; if you don't you can actually cause more problems. Learn to give a very deep and satisfying massage and then each of you takes about 5 or 10 minutes to massage each other before you think about sex. Not only are you really getting in the mood but you will be helping each other to breathe properly and to relax. Foot and back messages are perfect for priming you for pleasure and comfort and, think of it this way – each minute you spend intimately massaging your partner is another minute towards your goal of lasting longer in bed.

3.   Take it in turns

Most sexual sessions are pretty much a give and take pleasure method, in which each of you touches each other at the same time, which means you are both heading for the finish line pretty darn quick. There is a golden rule here if you really want things to take longer – take it in turns to touch each other. From now on, let your partner do the touching while you relax, lie back and take as much pleasure from it as you can without getting too over-excited. Then return the favor; let her lie back while you do the touching and exploring. Both of you need to learn how to use your hands properly to give as much pleasure as possible, leading both of you down the road to arousal but not so quick as it would normally happen.

4.   Control your surroundings

The truth of the matter is when you are in a comfortable position, in comfortable surroundings, a place where either you or your partner is likely to get too over excited, you are more likely to last longer in bed. Don't be tempted with public sex or anything else that could be just that little too exciting for you. If your most comfortable place for sex is in bed then keep it in the bedroom, at least until you have learned how to control your orgasm.

5.   Woman on top

I mentioned this one earlier; by having the woman on top, you don't feel so stimulated. Plus, ask her to take it slowly. Long, hard and fast thrusts are pretty dangerous for a man on the edge! You could also try penetrating her and then not moving for a couple of minutes, just to let yourself get acclimatized to her.

6.   Use the start-stop technique

With this technique, your woman will stimulate you until you start to get close to an orgasm. At this point, tell her that she must stop. When your levels of sexual tension have reduced, it could be as quick as 15 seconds, start again. By doing this frequently, not only will you last longer for that particular session but you will also begin to understand your own feelings and will learn how to stop yourself.

7.   Learn to breathe from the belly

When you breathe deeply, it is actually a direct correlation to ejaculation. So, breathing deeply and slowly should help you to reduce stress and anxiety, thus slowing down your rate of ejaculation. Learn how to breathe so that your belly will rise before your chest does and practice this in conjunction with the start-stop technique. You could also practice the yoga breathing technique I told you about earlier.

8.   Read the Kama Sutra

Preferably together as this will heighten the pleasure for both of you. Plus, you could always try out some of the positions! In all seriousness, though, there is a specific technique that is mentioned that can help you to stay the distance. Using this technique, start off very slowly, with just one in and out stroke per three seconds. Then you can begin to build up the strokes, adding in more, over a session of about four or five minutes until you are at the stage where you are giving one stroke per second. If you feel as if you are about to lose control, stop, stay inside your woman until you regain control and then start from the beginning again

9.   Out of your head

And I do not mean on drugs or alcohol! One of the biggest killers during sex, the one thing that will affect whether you can maintain an erection or not, is stress. And that comes down to what is going through your mind. In the case of premature ejaculation or in those who seem to rush it all the time, the main thoughts are going to be on your abilities and your performance and that will likely push you over the edge. Learn how to change your thinking to positivity and confidence pushing worry and stress out of the way. If you start to feel anxious or stressed during sex, stop, breathe deeply and then focus on your inner self. Get rid of the negative thoughts and put your attention firmly on you and your feelings.

10.   Try new positions

I gave you five positions to try earlier to help you last longer in bed but you could always open that copy of the Kama Sutra. There are specific positions that are designed to make your orgasm happen quicker and others, like the ones I told you about that will prolong things. Experiment, try a few out and see what works and what doesn't.

11.   Learn to control your ejaculatory muscle

When you ejaculate, do you ever wonder what physically causes it to happen? There is a specific muscle that controls your ejaculation and, when it is relaxed, you simply cannot ejaculate, no matter how hard you try. We talked about it earlier – it's called the PC muscle and it what is responsible for letting the semen come out when you come. To control your rate of ejaculation, you have to know how to control this muscle. Practice the exercises we talked about earlier as much as you can until you have almost full control over it. This won't be instant; it can take as much as four weeks to get really good results. It will also take a great deal of regular practice to get it right and become a sexual master.

12   Learn to control your confidence and mental health

Back in the olden days, it used to be thought that premature ejaculation was the result of mental health problems and men who suffered from it were immediately sent for hypnotherapy or to see a psychiatrist. Obviously neither of those worked very well. While premature ejaculation is a physical condition, it is also linked to mental health and this must not be ignored. You must learn how to manage your concentration levels, your thoughts, and your confidence levels while you are having sex. If you don't, it will have a serious effect on how long you can manage to last for.

13.   Masturbate often

If you truly want to know how to last a long as possible between the sheets, you need to get more in tune with your own sexual responses. To do that, you're going to have to masturbate more. When you begin to stimulate yourself, make sure that you stop before you can't. Let's say that, on a scale of 1 to 10, the orgasm is number 10. So stop yourself at about 8. Make sure you leave time to calm down and then start again, working your way back up that scale. Do this as often as you need to in order to learn how to control yourself.

14.   Learn how to cool down

Whether you suffer from premature ejaculation or not, you should still learn a few methods for cooling down. You can practice these so that, if you do find yourself heading towards being out of control you can stop yourself before you do go over the edge. Do your research and find the methods that will work for you, that will help you to last a bit longer in bed.

15.   Change it up

What is the absolute best thing you can do when you find yourself heading fast toward that point of no return? The biggest piece of advice that I can give you is to change your speed. Men should have a go at teasing their partners; remove your tool from inside her and rub the head up and down over her sex. There are a lot of nerve endings there and this will make her feel great, as well as help to slow you down a bit.

16.   Squeeze

Earlier on, we mentioned the most sensitive parts of the penis. There are three areas that, when squeezed, can help to slow you down and keep you hard. First, when your penis is erect, make a ring with your index finger and your thumb around the base of it and squeeze it. This stimulates a ring around the base of the penis which helps to keep the blood where it should be. The second place is underneath the head of the penis. Applying pressure there can work wonders as it is the hot spot in most men and is full of nerve endings. Lastly, the perineum, the spot that is located in between the anus and the base of your testicles.

All of these techniques are designed for you, with you in mind. Basically, do whatever it takes to make your bedtime sessions last as long as you both want them to.

There is something here that I must reiterate. You may think that it is OK to go for hours in bed and that maybe what you are aiming for. Please don't. Unless your partner is a machine or made of some other substance than blood, skin, and bone, it isn't wise or pleasurable to make sex last for a prolonged period of time, especially not the penetration part of it. It can be painful and uncomfortable, not just for your woman but for you too. Too much thrusting away can cause lubrication to dry up and then it becomes less of the pleasure and much more of the pain. You aren't in the movies and you don't need to perform for the cameras, just for you and her.

Different Sex Positions In A Relationship

Sex and sex positions

Sex might mean different things to different people but the bottom line is that it is a very healthy and natural activity that everyone enjoys and find meaningful even with all the different meaning by different people. Sex is not just about vaginal intercourse; sex can be anything that feels sexual which could be vaginal sex, anal sex, hugging, kissing, oral sex or any sexual touching. Sexual activities are very important in a relationship whether one is straight, a lesbian, and bisexual, queer or gay or in any kind of sexual relationship. So basically, sex is any sexual activities that we engage in with our partners for sexual pleasure and gratification. We all know that there will come a time that it might become boring or like a routine if we do not spice things up and this is where sex positions come into play.

Sex positions are the different sultry styles and ways of having orgasmic sex, sex positions should be used just like outfits where different ones should be used at different times. Imagine having sex that makes it looks like you are in your honey moon stage all the time. This is possible if you are acquainted with all the sex positions and its techniques. The fact is that with this, you wouldn't be able to keep your hands away from each other.

·   Tips and tricks to help you love adventurous sex positions

It is one thing is to know about the different hot pleasurable sex positions and orgasmic thrilling styles that can be adopted in the bedroom but the hardest part is being in the mood to explore and to try the suggestions and the new ideas out. The fact is that stepping up and trying something new might be terrifying, scary or uncomfortable for you but there are a lot of ways you can help raise yourself to your sexual height to stop sex drought. If you always need loud moaning, the bed squeaking and having passion sex with your partner then you need to use and love different sex positions. Because it is only this way that you will be able to heighten the fire, the excitement, passion and mind-blowing orgasm that have diminished in your sex life. So to rediscover your lost sexual desires and yearning for having sizzling sex. You can follow the under listed tricks and tips to get yourself to always be in a best mood for new steaming sexual positions.

·   Get yourself a sexy masseur or masseuse

So you can get yourself in the mood by first wearing a kinky or sexy stuff to be more attractive, and then ask your partner to use hot oils to give you good soothing massages all over the body. This will help to reduce tension and as tension reduces from all part of your muscles, it will put you in a better mood to try your new sultry sex suggestions and positions.

- Keep installing the sex ideas in your mind

You will find yourself horny and needing good sex when you keep seeing an erotic sex picture in advance and how you will be having explosive sex under the sheet when you try out some very kinky sex positions. Make some noises, say sensual things and whisper sweet nothings in your partner ears ahead of time. Just go all naughty with your partner and talk dirty to prepare your mind for some very crazy sex positions that you will be expecting from your partner in the bedroom. All these will add up and make you want to try out hot sex positions and be in love with them.

- Spring up a surprise anywhere

There is something sensual and steamy about having a surprise sex anywhere else in the house especially in the shower and a lot of couples likes sexual encounters in the shower, so you can skip the boring bedroom routine for the time being and try other places and most importantly the shower. Surprise your partner maybe in the shower with erotic kisses, demand some fingering from your partner and totally move your hands all over your partner's body and let your partner's reciprocate same till you get in the mood.

· Flirt and play around with your partner

You can get yourself in the mood for some kinky sex in advance by sending suggestive but subtle text messages to your partner to let him or her know what's on your mind. You can flirt with sending romantic and sex appeal messages to their phone; you can also sound naughty and dirty as possible to give them a clue about your moves. All of these will add to make your sexual advances more persuasive and alluring to your partner and they will respond in a crazy way that will put you in the kind of sex mood you needed.

· Take the initial sex initiative

No need waiting for your partner to be in sexual mood by his or her self, because this route might take longer than you thought. Your partner might not be vocal about it but he or she will definitely appreciate if you take the bold step. You need to supercharge in the bedroom and then create a sexy atmosphere around your partner, he or she would feel aroused and attracted to your body. So go ahead and let them know you are really for sex with them and introduce the sex position you want to try out.

· Introduce porn videos

This could be the key you need to arouse yourself and be in the mood for a new sex position. Porn videos helps to introduce new sizzling sex positions and how to use them, there are a lot of porn videos now you can stream online or download to watch, just get the ones in accordance with your sex fantasies and you can watch it with your partner together. Watching the porn videos together can instantly arouse your partner and you both can practicalize what you are watching or just watched immediately, this will even help to make the experience more adventurous.

· Raise your self confidence

Sometimes you might feel insecure and may have low self esteem and this might lead to you not having physical connection with your partner. You will need to work on this aspect of your sexual life. so you need to remind him constantly that you have a banging body, that your partner will still find your body irresistible and hot, apparently, you need to keep arousing him or her with hot kisses, fondling, cuddling etc. to make them feel desirable by you too. So all these will help you be desirable by partner and your partner will also be irresistible to you too and which will open you up to try out the new sex positions you have in your head.

Outstanding gains of using different sex positions in a relationship

If all you think is a kiss and quickie after a long day of work that will just satisfy your partner, then you are in Lalaland because your partner thinks sex with you is very boring. Your sex life should be explosive that of fun, passion, multiple orgasm and thrills. Your bedmatics skills should be hot and irresistible that your partner will love and be eager to be part of, and as such it always good to spice up your sex life to ignite the gone chemistry or heightened the passion that already exist. So, it is expedient for you and your partner to learn how to unstuck from a sexual routine that must have engulf your sex lives. Give different sex positions a shot to kill boredom that will aid to spark the sexual flames and ignite all the intense feelings for love making. You might not have known but the below points are some killer reasons why you should learn and try out different sex positions in your sex life.

· 	It will emotionally connect you both

Nothing beats the good old benefits of emotionally connection with a partner after having fantastic bomb sex with one another. You two will stay connected to one another; there will be this subjective feeling that will bond both of you together. This kind of connection will help to arouse strong feelings which will enable you to value mind and soul of your partner and makes you have deep and meaningful conversations with them.

·   It will increase intimacy

Introducing new sex positions in the bedroom all the time will keep away unfriendliness and aloofness from partners, so to have a moment of greatest pleasure or rush of sexual excitement with your partner. You must know how to keep things spicy and hot in the bedroom. Good amount of intimacy is needed to keep the connection very strong.

·   It offers immense sexual pleasure

Working with some new ideas and sexual suggestions will make you and your partner rediscover your selves, this is like finding the best options that will build on already existing pleasurable zones. By trying new sex position you will discover more pleasurable options you will have to explore and of course the end result is more excitement and enjoyment during sex et al. Again, this will enhance deep penetration for the man and a better thrusting for the woman and these add up to make the sex experience heavenly. This is like finding both G-spot and what can give you both the ultimate satisfaction.

· Easy orgasm for the partners

Nothing is as frustrating as not being able to climax, in fact it shouldn't have a place in your bedroom or a very abnormal thing to experience. I believe orgasm is an experience that no couples want to exclude from their sex session because this is the explosive part of love making and it helps couples to love themselves better after a wow sex session. So using different sex positions in the bedroom can actual help you achieve this explosion effortlessly. It is all about going with the ideal positions and ideas that will give the best result. Of course if one doesn't experiment with the sultry positions learned, it might be counter-productive if one only gets to know about them without exploring and experimenting with them.

· It makes couples to be flexible

Knowing different sex positions and willingly to use them enable you to have several and numerous sex options to explore. Switching things up in the bedroom using the different sexual suggestions provided here will help spice up things in the bedroom. This will help you and your partner stop seeing sex as a routine or chore that needs to be done for the sake of it but what they look forward to having for immense pleasure, getting freaky and exploring another pleasurable zones. Using different sex positions available will make sex for couples or partners be more of a necessity and what should be done to make life more alluring for partners.

Conclusion

Sex is an important part of life and crucial for being in a fulfilling relationship. Whether you have a great sex life and just want to keep experimenting, or you're just starting to explore what makes you and your partner feel good, I hope this guide has been a useful resource for you. By opening up communication with your partner about sex, you can both continue to explore and grow sexually, figuring out how to have the most satisfying sexual relationship possible. Sex is for everyone, from flexible yogis to couch potatoes, so wink at your partner, shimmy out of your clothes, and start having fun!

There is so much to explore, so many parts of our human psyche that are still untapped, waiting for the right key to come unlock them. I believe that almost anyone can be consumed by the allure sex poses. It becomes a challenge to reach certain milestones – losing your virginity, receiving your first oral sex, giving your first oral sex, having sex in public for the first time, trying your first sex toy, making love for the first time. It's fun. There's also a certain amount of ego involved. It feels good to be doing this stuff, and I do think that sex is a fundamental need we have as human beings.

But it's also important not to place too much emphasis on your "success" or "failure" in this conquest. I have been through periods where I was not having any sex, and for whatever reason, I let it affect my self-esteem and my sense of self-worth. This is an unhealthy view of sexuality. You are letting your mind become vulnerable to an outside force that can be largely out of your control. The conquest should not be a conquest at all. There should not be anything to conquer, or to do better than someone else, or to do before someone else.

It should be an exploration of this aspect of life. You should try your best to seek the truth in your sex life. Find out what you truly want. Find a partner or partners who share your desires.

Make the most of those experiences. Don't do this for personal gain or to make yourself feel better. Don't do it to selfishly "get yourself off."

Do it to genuinely share a unique connection with someone.

Do it to have the most fun you possibly can.

I mean, that's what this is all about right? Having a good time?

So, take what you have learned here, go forth in your sex life with confidence and determination to find that truth which only you can find.

www.ingramcontent.com/pod-product-compliance
Lightning Source LLC
LaVergne TN
LVHW012129060726
842759LV00027B/583